Images of Spain

IMAGES OF SPAIN

Photographs by Peter Christopher
Text by Mordecai Richler

McClelland and Stewart

Contents

Page 5

Spain is bounded by three seas – Biscay, the Atlantic, and the Mediterranean. From the Portuguese border to Tarifa, the Spanish coast is known as the Costa de la Luz, or Coast of Light, celebrated for its exquisite sandy beaches. Tarifa, the country's most southern town, is less than 13.5 km from Africa, across the Straits of Gibraltar. It was named after the Berber Tarif Ibn Malluk, who led one of the first Muslim raids into Spain in 710. Cádiz, the largest port on the coast, was settled by the Phoenicians. Nelson's body was sent home from Cádiz, embalmed in a Domecq sherry butt.

Page 7

Stream flowing out of Laguna Negra de Urbión (Black Lagoon of the Urbión Sierra) in the province of Soria. Part of the Iberian Cordillera, the lagoon is actually a glacial lake in the Sierra Urbión which rises to 2228 m. Astonishing as it may seem, the snows in the higher peaks of the Pyrenees and Baetic chains are eternal.

Page 9

The Yesa Reservoir is one of the highest in Europe. South of the Pyrenees, in one of the driest, and therefore least productive, chunks of the country, it is fed by the Aragón River. Tiermas, the village nestling at the top of the mountain on the left, as well as Ruesta, the one on the far shore, were both abandoned when the lake was formed. Tiermas was the site of an old Roman spa, now flooded.

Page 11

Burning wheat stubble in La Mancha. *Manxa* means parched earth in Arabic. Even so, this high tableland is the country's largest wine-producing region. Olive trees also flourish here; so do certain grain crops. But, alas, there are very few windmills left in the land of Sancho Panza and the Knight of the Sorrowful Countenance.

Page 12

Wildflowers in a field north of Córdoba. In this land of spring flowers, they compare the region in bloom to a *novia*–a girl betrothed.

Last November, after an absence of twenty-five years, I finally returned to Spain.

Turbulent Spain.

"That country nipped off from hot Africa," as Auden wrote, "soldered so crudely to inventive Europe."

Putting the snows of Montreal behind us, my wife and I flew to Madrid. It was, for my wife, a first trip. A fresh experience. But, for me, it was a voyage undertaken with longing and apprehension. Once, Spain had fascinated me. However, when I was twenty years old, I had also thought it would be unfair to bring children into a post-Hiroshima world and that the novel was dead. Now I am the father of five and earn my living as a novelist.

I first saw Madrid in 1952, during Semana Santa. Semana Santa, the eight days of Holy Week, beginning with Palm Sunday, once had a frightening power in Madrid; the procession, as I recall it, arousing more terror than religious awe. All around me, people sank to their knees, crossing themselves, as a litter bearing Christ on the Cross passed, the gorier aspects of the crucifixion emphasized. Here, even as in the bullfight, the Spanish obsession with blood. Lorca wrote,

> *¿Qué sientes en tu boca*
> *roja y sedienta?*
> *El sabor de los huesos*
> *de mi gran calavera.*

> What is it you feel
> in your red, thirsty mouth?
> The taste of the bones
> of my big skull.

Following, there rode a battalion of grim soldiers mounted on white horses; they wore *Wehrmacht*-type battle helmets and blew mournfully on trumpets. Then came the penitents. Masked, wearing tall pointed hats and red or black robes, many of them barefoot.

In 1952, long before prosperity had struck, Madrid was still slumbering, nursing the wounds of grievances of civil war, a quaint backwater in a resurgent Europe. Why, in those days I remember that calumny was to call somebody a freemason. Even monarchists, among them the red-haired Luisa María, Duchess of Valencia, were imprisoned from time to time. Once, when the duchess was to be briefly incarcerated in Las Ventas, a women's prison on the outskirts of Madrid, her butler waited at the gates with her prison kit, which included cologne water and salmon silk pajamas. Now, not only had the monarchy been restored, but the communist party was on the brink of being legalized.

Some twenty-five years ago the most magnificent bullfighter in the country, Luis Miguel Dominguín, had been arrested for running off with the nineteen-year-old daughter of a grandee of Spain, the Duke Carlos Pérez Soane de Pino Hermoso. "I like Dominguín," the duke explained. "He has the heart of a lion and the legs of a deer. What's more, he will probably end up much richer than I am. But there is one thing I simply cannot change – his family."

In those days, I should point out, no respectable woman was to be seen without an escort even in the most stylish bar, but now the newly liberated daughters of the middle-class actually smoked on the streets, slouching down the Gran Vía in jeans. Once, the city shut down tight at one P.M., not opening again until four, everybody going home for a siesta, but now, I was assured, "Hardly anybody goes home between two and four any more, there's no time, especially in this traffic." The quick lunch had come in, heralded by the Hamburger King. Today the thrusting, heavily industrialized city spilled over into ugly suburbs, even as any North American metropolis. Where once there were hardly any cars whatsoever, the rush hour traffic now seemed endless.

Madrid, Madrid.

It is the highest of European capitals, nestled in the Sierras, lying in the very centre of Spain, the hub of a wheel whose spokes lead to mountains deep in snow or desertland or an endless roll of olive groves. To Navarre, Asturias, Extremadura, La Mancha, Andalusia and Catalonia. If it is not, by any reckoning, the most visually enchanting of European capitals, the inferior by far to Paris or Rome, it may well be the most vibrant.

"The Spaniards are, by nature, short of stature, with a dark skin that is rough from dryness," wrote a perspicacious seventeenth-century traveller, Barthelemy Joly, in his *Voyage en Espagne.* "Their houses, *luteae domus!*

(houses of mourning), are usually nothing but three small, interconnected rooms, without study or cabinet, and so uncomfortable and poorly furnished that they seem built not to be inhabited. There is no place there to maintain privacy. For that reason they are rarely at home, and when they go out it is to stroll in the squares and talk in groups that are called *corrillos.*"

Madrileños, at least the very rich and the new, burgeoning middle-class, no longer live in houses of mourning, but, happily, they still take to the streets at all hours. I have, come to think of it, never known the streets of Madrid or any other Spanish town when they were not swarming with animated people, the stream all but impassable in the early evening when thousands are out for their *paseo.* Taking *tapas* in a succession of *tascas,* each one boasting its own speciality.

Tapas are *hors d'oeuvres,* usually eaten early in the evening with a beer or a *chato,* a small glass of red wine, and meant to stay you until dinner, seldom served before ten. Beware of *calamares fritos,* which look like French fried onion rings, but taste suspiciously like elastic bands. *Champiñones fritos* fried in olive oil and garlic are something else. But the most delicious, beyond a doubt, are the *gambas a la plancha,* giant grilled shrimp in the shell.

Whatever the season Madrid abounds in fresh fish, trucked through the night from the Mediterranean ports. Sole, hake, bass, tuna, eels, barnacles, squid, shrimp, mussels, clams, and spider crab. As in Italy, the beef is best avoided, but there is fine partridge in the autumn, and on a frosty winter night there's nothing quite so gratifying as a *cocido madrileño,* that is to say, Madrid hotpot, superbly done at La Bola.

Built in 1860, La Bola is a typical, inexpensive *taberna* that includes Ava Gardner among its *aficionados. Cocido* is actually a two-course stew, served in an earthenware pot. The broth is served as a soup course and following that there is a variety of boiled chicken, stewing meat and sausages, bolstered with chick-peas and other vegetables. The Spanish version of *pot-au-feu.*

The best restaurant in Madrid, however, is also reputedly the oldest in Europe; I speak of Casa Botín, founded in 1725 and precisely two centuries later much-favoured by the young Ernest Hemingway. The currently unfashionable Mr. Hemingway was not only a fair country writer, he was also a man of taste. Casa Botín, with its low vaulted ceilings, cloister-like arches, blue-tiled walls and sinking marble floor, is not only a charming place to eat, it also offers fine food: *cochinillo asado,* roast suckling pig, or *cordero asado,* roasted side of baby lamb.

Spanish cuisine is largely a reflection of the taste of the country's conquerors. When the Phoenicians landed in Andalusia, in 600 B.C., they planted the first olive tree. Roman soldiers discovered the grape that yields sherry, and it was the Moorish invaders of the eighth century who planted the first orange and almond trees. *Paella,* the quintessential Spanish dish to some, is actually an adaptation of Persian pilaf. To be fair, however, it was the *conquistadores* themselves, back from plundering the New World, who returned not only with gold, but also with the humble potato. Hence, the *tortilla española* or Spanish omelet.

On arrival in Madrid, we had checked into the Ritz and taken breakfast in the grand, high-ceilinged dining room. Hanging tapestries on one side, immense French doors on the other, the walls painted a soft Mediterranean blue. From there, eschewing modern Madrid, we repaired to the Puerta del Sol, the symbolic heart of the city, Kilometre 0, the point from which all the main roads of the country radiate. It was then only a short walk to the perfectly made Plaza Mayor, which was exactly as I had remembered it. Its cobblestones nicely worn, its Herrera towers so lovely to contemplate, the porticoes perfection itself. Exhilarated, the largely sleepless night on Air Iberia shaken off, we sipped *aperitivos* and nibbled olives in the sun. Gypsy fortune-tellers worked the café tables. Here and there fathers booted a football around with their kids. Soldiers on leave photographed each other before the statue of Philip III. This being a Sunday morning the weekly stamp market was in full flutter, old men vying for position at makeshift tables, fishing magnifying glasses out of waistcoat pockets the better to scrutinize perforation marks.

Passing through the Cuchilleros Arch, down the narrow Cava de San Miguel, originally the moat on the other side of the square's mediaeval ramparts, we fell in with the throng heading for the Rastro, the fabled Madrid flea market, which flourishes on Sunday mornings on the Ribera de Curtidores. Survivors coming the other way, a thin trickle all but overwhelmed by the oncoming crowds, carried lamp shades, kettles, bolts of cloth. Others wheeled their acquisitions in rickety prams. A stout lady, holding a terrified canary in a cage aloft, pleaded for passage, unavailingly. A man, trying to carry away a moth-eaten easy chair overturned on his head, was swung one way and then another, in clear danger of toppling. Spinning, he cleared a space for himself, set his newly acquired chair down in the street in a cloud of dust, and settled into it defiantly, letting the others swirl around him. Walter Starkie, who visited the Rastro in 1934, wrote, "If Adam and Eve were again cast out of Paradise and dropped into the Plaza del Rastro they could descend the Ribera de Curtidores hand in hand and arrive at the bottom of the hill fully clothed, and they could set up house on the plain with the objects they had collected."

Were he to return today, Starkie would discover every conceivable item is still on sale in the stalls of the Rastro on Sunday mornings. Mantillas, canes, duelling pistols, swords, ancient irons, copper pots, broken fans, buttons, cassettes, souvenir *botas* and *porrones.* bullfight posters with your own name emblazoned thereon, silk top hats, and a plethora of garish dolls and paintings. For the rest, Starkie would obviously find Madrid vastly changed since 1934. There has, among other things, been a civil war. An embittering civil war. El Caudillo, Generalísimo Francisco Franco, outlasting Hitler, Mussolini and Stalin, has finally gone, leaving behind a country in a state of excitement mingled with apprehension.

"So far," a knowledgeable observer told me, "what we have is democracy with a parachute. We are only halfway there. We haven't landed safely yet."

Put plainly, what he feared was the resurgent if not yet quite legal communist party, easily the best organized political group in the country. The present leader of the communist party, Santiago Carrillo, may protest that he is committed to the democratic path to power, that he disapproves of internal repression in Russia and even accepts the presence of American bases in Spain, but not everybody is convinced. The Spanish, an inward-looking people consumed by an uncommonly bloody past, are given to cherishing old wounds. Carrillo's opponents have been dragging up his past. His civil war past.

When Carrillo was a mere twenty-one, in November 1936, and effectively in charge of public order in besieged, republican Madrid, several thousand nationalist prisoners were taken from their cells and disappeared. Nobody doubts that they were murdered, but there is less certainty about whether Carrillo actually ordered the slaughter. The shootings could have been started by trigger-happy guards. Carrillo protests that, with Franco's troops at the gates to the city, he ordered the prisoners transferred to Valencia. On the way, he says, "forces whose identity we were unable at the moment to establish took over the convoy and killed the prisoners, outside my jurisdiction...I accept responsibility for not taking a brigade from the front to protect the prisoners on the way to Valencia." But, at the time, he adds, his side was unable to spare even a single man.

It may be unfair, the Spanish correspondent for *The Economist* ventures, to resurrect a murky episode from a war that was extremely bloody on both sides to discredit a present-day political leader, but there are those who feel the communists (indeed, all parties) might best be served by a younger generation of leaders, men untainted by the brutalities of the civil war. To this Carrillo replies, "Only my generation, which fought in the civil war, [has] the moral and political authority to lead at this time."

Franco, who dominated Spanish life for forty years, was laid to rest in 1975 in the *Valle de los Caídos,* the Valley of the Fallen, where some 40,000 civil war dead had already been buried.

The Valley of the Fallen, an hour's ride out of Madrid, is bounded on the north by the parish of Guadarrama and on the south by the stream of Guatal. It commands a vista of extraordinary beauty, a natural cross formed by the Carpetana and Ibérica mountain chains. The site is dominated by a cross 300 metres high that soars out of an outcropping of bony brown mountain rock. Below, there is a church leading into a vast crypt hewn out of the mountain itself. The church is surrounded by a wide esplanade overlooking a rocky valley of pines, broom, oaks, and poplars. Alongside, there are gardens both elaborate and ornate and, behind, a monastery and, as an integral part of the monument, a centre of Catholic social studies. The official guide-book to the site notes, "the Monument is religious in character, because it is thus more in keeping with the simple piety of the Spanish people, who have remained outside the current of agnosticism which has secularized Europe in this century."

Not, to be sure, any more. The people who massacred Charlemagne's army in the pass of Roncesvalles, ultimately defeated the Moors and sent Napoleon's armies packing, has finally been overwhelmed by a new and absolutely unstoppable army of affluence, the tourists of northern Europe and America, who have brought with them news of the world beyond the Pyrenees, bikinis and transistor radios, yanking the Spaniards howling with astonishment into the twentieth century, the rushing mainstream of agnosticism and secularized Europe.

If, in 1952, foreign travellers were still a novelty in Spain, and in those days I found myself something of a curiosity wherever I wandered on the peninsula, today the tourist is ubiquitous. Camera-laden Japanese photograph each other in the gardens of the Alhambra. Come spring there appear to be more golden-haired Scandinavians in campers than windmills in La Mancha. There are stretches of the Costa del Sol, colonized by retired couples out of Esher and Leatherhead, where there is more English spoken than any other language, where tea and scones and even cucumber sandwiches have displaced the traditional *tapas*. Condominiums have shot up here, there, and everywhere to accommodate hordes of prospering Germans. And no sandy beach is complete without its Dutchman boiling in the sun.

But this is not to say that traditional, seemingly timeless Spain is no longer to be found, *even on Majorca.*

Majorca, the largest of the Balearics, may now very well be the island of cheap package tours, but its more inaccessible fishing villages have not changed much since George Sand lived there with Chopin. "We followed the right arm of the mountain-range," George Sand wrote in *Winter in Majorca* (1839), "climbing from hill to hill, up a stony path which cut our feet to pieces, until we reached the northern coast. At each turn of the path we saw the sea stretched out magnificently, far below us, and a belt of beautiful vegetation lying between us and it. I had never before seen such fertile shores, clothed with trees and shrubs down to the first wave, instead of the usual white cliffs, dreary salt flats or muddy beaches. In every part of the French coast that I know, even the heights of Port-Vendres, where at least I experienced its full beauty, I have always thought the sea dirty or disagreeable to approach. Even the famous Lido of Venice is a horribly bare stretch of sand, inhabited by huge lizards that dart out in thousands from under your feet and seem to be chasing you in ever increasing numbers, as in a nightmare. At Royant, at Marseilles, almost everywhere I believe on our coasts, a belt of sticky seaweed and a desert of sand spoil our approach to the sea. In Majorca alone I finally saw the sea of my dreams, clear and blue as the sky, like a sapphire plain carefully ploughed into gently undulating furrows which, if you are looking down from a certain height, seem quite still and framed by dark green forests. Every step on the winding mountain path offered us a new view, each more superb than the last."

I first saw Spain in the winter of 1951, grudgingly journeying down to Barcelona from civilized Paris, a young and unpublished writer, ridden with scurvy of all things, in disgruntled need of some sun on the cheap. I had intended to endure exile from the excitements of Montparnasse for no more than two weeks, but, to my astonishment, the country captured my heart. I remained rooted there, on the enchanting island of Ibiza, in the Balearics, for almost a year, venturing on to the peninsula again and again, for Semana Santa in Madrid, the diversions offered by Barcelona's raunchy *barrio chino* on any night of the year, and the *Fallas* in Valencia.

Ah, I remember Valencia, the *Fallas*, being twenty years old in the spring, an underachiever with holes in my socks and no plans for the future but more travel.

Valencia, lying on the banks of the Río Turia, is in the heart of the orange country, its fruit succulent beyond compare.

Founded by the Greeks, overrun in turn by the Carthaginians, the Romans, Visigoths, and Arabs, Valencia is, above all, the city of El Cid, the Campeador or Champion of Castile, more properly known as Rodrigo Diaz de Vivar. El Cid, leading an army of 7,000 men, mostly Muslims, captured Valencia after a bitter nine-month siege in 1094. And since then, no rumour of war, no insurrection, has come to Spain without touching the volatile port of Valencia.

In 1808, Valencia rose against the French. In 1843, there was yet another rebellion, this one to restore the regency of María Cristina of Naples. During the Spanish civil war, after the fall of Madrid, Valencia became the last stronghold of the tattered republican forces.

In 1952, you could still see destroyed or bomb-damaged buildings in the old town, but I had come for the *Fallas,* my first experience of a fiesta. I had also come, as it turned out, to see my first western dubbed in Spanish, big Joel Macrea moseying up to the saloon bar in Tombstone and demanding, *"Un coñac, por favor."*

Armed with Mr. Hemingway's *Death in the Afternoon,* my ticket to passing for an *aficionado,* I was eager to see Litri, Aparicio, and the young Luis Miguel Dominguín fight bulls, necessarily brave, in the Plaza de Toros. Having once studied Hemingway's splendid glossary, I had absorbed enough to holler *ianda!,* go on, at any picador who was reluctant to charge the bull, and *camelo,* or fake, at any bullfighter "who by tricks tries to appear to work close to the bull while in reality never taking any chances."

The fiesta was rooted in the Middle Ages when, on St. Joseph's Day, the carpenters' brotherhood burned their accumulated wood shavings in bonfires known as *fallas.* It is marked not only by *corridas,* but also by parades; madness the rule rather than the exception. Fantastic *papier-mâché* floats, most of them satiric in nature, are produced by different quarters of the town in fierce competition and paraded through the Plaza del Caudillo and the adjoining streets. Then, on the evening of March 19, everything goes up in flames.

Suddenly, as I recall it, all the street lights were extinguished and the fireworks display began.

A thin nervous line of red light shot up into the sky, ripping the darkness, exploding into shivering streaks of red and orange and green. Another scratch of light darted skywards, shattering itself in mid-air and momentarily illuminating the plaza in an eerie yellow light. The crowd sighed. Some people recoiling, others tittering. Soon the sky was exploding in multi-coloured grandeur, bleeding a myriad of trickling stars, shot through with gaping holes and oblique pin-lines of firecracker lights.

The giant *falla* of a pot-bellied gypsy burst into flames.

Another send-off of rocket lights wooshed upward, blossoming over the flames of the burning *falla,* spluttering and hissing, pumping more angry rents into the sky.

Still another flurry zoomed heavenwards, rattling, spluttering, dribbling coloured stars on the plaza, and then there were still more explosions, more lights, and all the other *fallas* went up in flames.

It was, to come clean, a far cry from the staid Queen Victoria Day celebrations of my boyhood, the only other fireworks display I was familiar with.

Yes, indeed.

And those flames in Valencia consumed not only a pot-bellied gypsy, after all, a stranger, but also a host of personal devils. The most wintry of my Canadian baggage as well as some of the more stultifying Jewish injunctions I had grown up with. Gone with the flames went the guilt acquired by leaving college without a degree. Not going on to medicine or law, which would have delighted my parents. Up with the smoke went the need to squirrel something away for a rainy day. The compulsion to be sensible above all. Into the ashes went the obligation to endure Canadian winters, simply because I had been born there. Or the necessity, this one more recently acquired, to understand *Finnegan's Wake* or adjudge myself shallow.

I'm a slow learner. But walking away from that fire I grasped, for the first time, that I was a free man. I owed no apologies. My life was mine to spend as I pleased.

The more liberating the drunk, the greater the hangover.

What, after all, was I doing in Spain, I wondered, even as I sailed back to Ibiza.

Coming from Canada, born to reticence in general and Montreal in particular, it seemed to me, even in those irresponsible days, that England and France, not to say the Babylonian Talmud, were a justifiable part of my heritage, but Spain, the country I had come to cherish, was utterly foreign. A dangerous indulgence.

I was only twenty then, impulsive, inexperienced, certainly not well travelled. Since 1952, however, I have lived in countries that certainly boasted more civilized forms of government, a more beneficial literary past, incomparably better food and wine, and yet – and yet – there remains to this day no land in Europe I find more compelling than Spain.

So it was exhilarating to be back, even on a tour unfortunately short, on that tableland, scored by rivers, that shelters beyond the Pyrenees, which shear it off from France.

Necessarily so, yes, for it was in Navarre, in the pass of Roncesvalles, that the fierce Basques massacred Charlemagne's army in 778; Roland leading its long and sorry retreat back through the Pyrenees into France.

For the French, the battle is celebrated in that country's first epic poem, the twelfth-century *Song of Roland,* a hymn for a handful of Christian knights resisting the Saracen hordes. But for the Spanish there is the poem of Bernardo del Carpio, the heroic tale of Bernardo the avenger, leading his bedraggled and outnumbered band of Basque, Navarrese, and Asturian patriots against the French invaders.

Each culture its own redeeming history, each society its own sweet arrogance.

Eskimaux, for instance, is really an Indian word, pejorative, meaning "eaters of raw meat." The truth is the Canadian Eskimos, no slouches, actually call themselves the Inuit, that is to say, The People, which puts the rest of us, Chosen or not, quite beyond the pale. Beasties born. And, according to Basque legend, Adam, the first gentleman, naturally spoke Basque, the language of angels. Furthermore, Richard Ford wrote in *Handbook for Spain,* the language "was brought pure into Spain, by Tubal, long before the confusion of tongues at Babel. Angelic or not, it was so difficult that the devil, who is no fool, is said to have studied seven years in the Bilboas, and to have learnt only three words."

Spain not only yielded to France the stuff of its first epic poem, but rendered to the rest of us the first proper novel, Miguel de Cervantes' masterpiece, *Don Quixote.*

> At a certain village in *La Mancha,* which I shall not name, there liv'd not long ago one of those old-fashion'd Gentlemen who are never without a Lance on a Rack, an old Target, a lean Horse, and a Greyhound. His Diet consisted more of Beef than Mutton; and with minc'd Meat on most Nights, Lentils on *Fridays,* Eggs and Bacon on *Saturdays,* and a Pigeon extraordinary on *Sundays,* he consumed three Quarters of his Revenue: The rest was laid out in a Plush-Coat, Velvet-Breeches, with Slippers of the same, for Holidays; and a Suit of the very best home-spun Cloth, which he bestowed on himself for Working-days. His whole Family was a Housekeeper something turn'd of Forty, a Niece not Twenty, and a Man that serv'd him in the House and in the Field, and could saddle a Horse, and handle the Pruning-hook. The Master himself was nigh fifty years of Age, of hale and strong Complexion, lean-body'd, and thin-fac'd, an early Riser, and a Lover of Hunting. Some say his Sirname was *Quixada,* or *Quesada* (for Authors differ in this Particular); However we may reasonably conjecture he was called *Quixada* (i.e., Lanthorn-Jaws) tho' this concerns us but little, provided we keep strictly to the Truth in every point of this History.
>
> You must know then, that when our Gentleman had nothing to do (which was almost all the Year round) he pass'd his Time reading Books of Knight-Errandry...

Seneca the Elder and his son, Lucius Seneca, both sprung from Spain, from Córdoba, to be precise, as did the Moorish physicist, astrologer, and mathematician, Averroës, and the great Jewish philosopher, Moses

Maimonides. Serious readers of fiction will be familiar with Spain's towering nineteenth-century novelist of manners, Pérez Galdos. In our own time there was Ortega y Gassett and the poetry and dramas of Federico García Lorca, the latter murdered by the nationalists during the civil war. But Lope de Vega doesn't travel well. Neither does Blasco Ibáñez. I cannot pretend that our debt to Spain is a literary one.

The Spanish genius, from Velázquez, Goya and El Greco, all the way through to Picasso, has really been for painting and architecture.

When Simone de Beauvoir first journeyed to America, in the fifties, she found the reality of that continent disconcerting, too much to conjure with, and again and again was driven back into the movie houses, if only to retrieve her first perception of that country, acquired as a young girl in the balconies of the cinemas of the *rive-gauche.* Footloose in Madrid, my wife and I, searching for an altogether more veracious and exacting mirror, found ourselves wandering through the Prado almost every morning.

Put plainly, I feel that any extended comment on this magnificent museum would be redundant, save to say it houses one of the greatest collections of art in the western world. Here hang the essential El Grecos, the best of Velázquez and Goya. One look at Goya's *Saturn Devouring His Son* and we grasp that Francis Bacon may just have deeper roots in Castile than the Home Counties. Goya's *El Tres de Mayo* (The Executions of the Third of May) explains a good deal about the country's bloody past. On May 2, 1808, crowds gathered before the palace in Madrid to prevent the departure of the queen and her children to Bayonne. Murat, the French general whose troops had occupied Madrid for two months, had ordered the royal banishment. Immediately, he found himself confronted by the insurrection which presaged the War of Independence. The Spaniards, led by Pedro Velarde, rose in revolt, an uprising that was cruelly suppressed by Murat the following morning, the patriots being executed on Principe Pío Hill in a dawn fusillade. According to tradition, Goya, accompanied by his servant, was present at the executions in the outskirts of Madrid, and the result was the two harrowing canvases which now hang in the Prado, *El Dos de Mayo* and *El Tres de Mayo.*

Eschewing modern Madrid, we were delighted to discover there were still cafés in the old town, say the Cervecería Alemana on the Plaza Santa Ana, actually an old bullfighter's haunt, which had not changed much over the years.

The Cervecería Alemana is a not so clean, but well-lighted, place, convenient to the Victoria Hotel, where some of the fighters and their managers and agents and camp followers still put up when they are in town for a *corrida.* Sides of *jamón serrano,* mountain ham, cured in the sun and snow, rock in the window and fading photographs of old bullfighters line the wood-panelled walls.

"The bullfight," Hemingway wrote, "is not a sport in the Anglo-Saxon sense of the word, that is, it is not an equal contest or an attempt at an equal contest between a bull and a man. Rather it is a tragedy; the death of the bull, which is played, more or less well, by the bull and the man involved in which there is danger for the man but certain death for the animal."

The bravest bulls have sprung from the ranches of Andalusia. So have the greatest bullfighters.

Belmonte, Joselito, Manolete.

Juan Belmonte, a peddler's boy born on the wrong side of the Guadalquivir River in Seville, was celebrated not so much for his style as for his incredible courage; he worked closer to the bull than anybody had before. Even so, to the astonishment of many an *aficionado,* Belmonte lived to the age of seventy, dying in bed.

Joselito was not so lucky, neither was Manolete.

Joselito, Belmonte's great rival, dominated Spain's *fiesta brava* in years leading up to and including the First World War. The son, nephew, and brother of a bullfighter, he began his career at the age of twelve, and celebrated his sixteenth birthday by killing six three-year-old bulls by himself. A matador of fabled poise and artistry, he was killed by a bull called Bailador on May 16, 1920, in the town of Talavera de la Reina.

Until the emergence of Manolete, in the summer of 1939, after the civil war had ended, there was nobody to challenge the memory of Belmonte or Joselito. The sad and melancholy Manolete, dubbed "The Knight of the Sorrowful Countenance" by the critics, dominated the *corrida* for seven years, until his tragic death after a fight in Linares in 1947.

Since then there has been Luis Miguel Dominguín and, more recently, the flashy El Cordobes, whom many took to be a vulgarian.

Never apologize, never explain.

There is no pardoning the cruel ritual of the bullfight, especially to horse-lovers, but as Mr. Hemingway once observed, after watching Algabeno work with the cape at a *corrida* in Pamplona (perfectly, graceful, debonair), "there was never such a scene in any world series game." Or, I might add, in any Stanley Cup Final either.

Put another way, though I've been to the Stanley Cup finals many times, I've never known a kid frisky enough to jump over the boards, hockey stick in hand, and sail in over the blue line to confront Bernie Parent or Roggie Vachon. But, watching my first bullfight in Valencia in 1952, I suddenly did see a scrawny boy, two rows down, leap from his seat, vault the *barrera,* broomstick and sack in hand, and make it clear on to the sands of the bullring, stamping his foot for the bull to charge. Around me people were cheering or laughing warmly, but I remember watching the boy, my heart hammering, until attendants hustled him off. I did not yet know that these boys, called *espontáneos,* were commonplace, and that I would see them again and again.

A corrida is made up of two kills each by three matadors. The spectacle begins with the band playing a rousing *paso-doble* to herald the entry of two mounted *alguaciles,* attendants of the corrida president in seventeenth-century costume. They are followed by the three matadors, leading their team of *picadores* and *banderilleros.* Each matador is adorned in his suit of light.

The matador's team, or *cuadrilla,* consists of *picadores* and *banderilleros.* The pike-wielding *picadores,* the first to treat with the bull, thrust their weapons into its withers as he charges, breaking the animal's speed and revealing its prowess and valour. They can be clumsy and cunning as well, sometimes thrusting too deep, weakening the bull beyond the call of decency. Next come the more elegant *banderilleros,* confronting the charging bull on foot, thrusting pairs, usually three, of brightly beribboned darts into the enraged animal.

Trumpet calls resound and now all is ready for the matador, his work with the *muleta, la faena de muleta,* and, ultimately, the sword, the *estocada.*

Striding into the arena, the matador salutes the president, dedicates his bull, usually to an honoured guest, flings his hat aside, and takes on the beast alone, with only a sword held in his right hand and a cape in his left. If, God help him, the matador makes a clumsy or timorous show with his *muleta,* or fails to drive his sword home properly for a clean kill, the president may wave his green handkerchief, the ultimate insult, allowing the bull to leave the arena alive. But if the matador performs with grace and skill, and the bull is brave, the president will bring out his blue handkerchief, a signal for mules to drag the carcass on a lap of honour. The matador, for his part, may be awarded the ears and the tail.

First, however, the matador must stand out there in the sand and make his passes; and, finally, as the bull stands still, head lowered, advance on him, aiming his sword between the shoulder blades, even as he distracts him with the *muleta.*

Bullfighting, as we have come to know it, began in Ronda, during the early eighteenth century: discovered by accident, born of necessity.

The town of Ronda nests on the top of a 200-metre ravine, in Andalusia, a short run from Malaga and the Costa del Sol, on one side, and Jerez de la Frontera, on the other. Between wars or voyages of conquest, its noblemen used to fight off ennui and, incidently, prove their valour by killing wild bulls from horseback in the grounds of the Royal Riding Circle. According to legend, one day shortly after the year 1700, a nobleman was upended by a bull's charge and lay pinned on the ground under his mount, helpless before the horns of the unrushing bull. Suddenly, one of the village poor, watching the spectacle, leaped into the ring and, using his flat-brimmed Andalusian hat as a lure, distracted the bull, leading him clear of the helpless nobleman. Then, to the astonishment and delight of the other onlookers, he continued to wave and manipulate his hat, teasing the bull, allowing him to rush past his body again and again.

The intrepid stranger was Francisco Romero, a carpenter's assistant, and he went on to introduce the *muleta,* lay down rules, and become the father of bullfighting. His son, Juan, introduced even more refinements, including the *cuadrilla,* and his grandson, Pedro, became one of the country's first great matadors, and the founder of the Ronda school, celebrated for its strict adherence to the rules of classicism.

From Madrid, we repaired to Toledo.

Caught shimmering in the sun on that rocky ridge that rises over the Tagus, Toledo is, quite simply, one of the most splendid sights in Europe. Within the city gates, its steep and narrow streets, buildings in the Gothic, "Mudéjar," Renaissance, and Baroque style, is a distillation of Arab, Jewish, and Christian history. Toledo remains, I suppose, the essence of Spain, turbulent Spain, from the time of the Visigoth kings, through the Moorish conquest and the Inquisition, to the civil war itself, when the massive Alcázar, dominating the city, destroyed and rebuilt so many times, was the scene of a famous siege, one of the legends of the war. In 1936, republican forces held Toledo under siege for seventy-two days, un-availingly, the nationalists standing fast. Colonel Moscardó, in command of the nationalists, was ordered by phone to surrender or see his son shot. He refused, and Luis Moscardó died on August 23. A month later a nationalist column broke the blockade, liberating the survivors holding out in the all but destroyed Alcázar.

The once celebrated Jewish quarter of Toledo, the *Judería,* extending to the edge of the cliff over the winding Tagus, was bounded from the north to south by the Cambrón Gate and the height of Montichel, now known as the Paseo de San Cristóbal. While the quarter flourished during the Middle Ages, before the expulsion of the Sephardic Jews by King Ferdinand and Queen Isabella, it was the home of the famous School of Translators, a brilliant centre of encyclopaedic culture, and the Plaza de la Judería was a thriving marketplace. Here you could buy Persian carpets, silks from Damascus, Indian pearls, Arabian perfumes, cloth from Kashmir, and spices from Ceylon. Then, something wicked that way came. The Inquisition. *Auto-de-fé.*

By a papal brief of February 11, 1482, among seven new Inquisitors nominated, there was the notorious Tomás de Torquemada, the Queen's confessor. Tribunals were swiftly organized in Jaén, Ciudad Real, and Córdoba; and in 1485, the seat of the Tribunal was transferred to Toledo. Here the *conversos,* Jews who had been forcibly converted, many continuing to practise their faith in secret, were both numerous and wealthy and they plotted to undo the Tribunal. They planned to rise during the Corpus Christi procession, killing the Inquisitors during the disorder. Furthermore, they even intended to seize the city gates and the tower of the Cathedral, holding it against the Crown. But their plot was betrayed, and on February 12, 1486, the first *auto* was held. Seven hundred and fifty Jews were forced to march barefoot and bareheaded through the streets of Toledo, carrying unlighted tapers and surrounded by an enraged mob. Their foreheads were marked with the words, "Receive the sign of the Cross which ye have denied and lost." They were fined, stripped of their civil rights, and compelled to march on six Fridays in succession, flagellating themselves with hempen cords. Before the year was done, more than 5,000 *conversos* were ordered to appear before the Tribunal. Many of them were burnt at the stake.

Hans Christian Andersen, a visitor to the twelfth-century Santa María la Blanca Synagogue in Toledo, in 1862, wrote, "This was the Jewish quarter, once the wealthiest part of the town. Spain's richest Israelites lived here and indeed, according to one legend, they built Toledo. What is certain, however, is that in this place and for a long time they enjoyed many more privileges than anywhere else. They were allowed to build a number of synagogues which look insignificant outside, but inside are glowing with richness and splendour. Two of them still remain as Christian churches, *Nuestra Señor del Tránsito* and *Santa María la Blanca*. The last is the more beautiful, a temple of God with Salomonic splendour. In the filigree, carved walls, which look like fine embroidery, are entwined Hebrew inscriptions, the lovely capitals of the pillars rise in horseshoe arches, light and airy. The temple stands here still but the people of Israel have gone; the buildings around, once so well-appointed, lie in ruins, and tenement-like hovels have sprung up in their place. Bright lizards, streaked with gold and other colours, dart in and out of their hiding places in this memory-rich ground. Here the people of Israel lived in their faith and customs, here they were for a time tolerated, but the days of tribulation came and they were shamefully dishonoured and tortured by the Christians."

But it is for the Corpus Christi Day procession, and not to mourn another Jewish culture past, that most visitors now come to incomparable Toledo.

Days beforehand the city begins to bedeck itself, preparing for that Thursday of splendour that, according to legend, "shines more than the sun." The narrow streets through which the procession will pass are covered with awnings that stretch from one side to another, in order to temper the heat of the light spring sun. Garlands made of pine branches adorn the route of the procession. Families decorate windows and balconies with tapestries, silk bedspreads and mantillas. Lavender, thyme, mint and other herbs are strewn on the pavement.

A mounted detachment of *guardia civil* leads the procession, followed hard by the kettle-drummers of the city hall and the processional cross of the cathedral. Then come children's choirs, bands, brotherhoods, priests, and the chapter of the cathedral. The Holy Sacrament. The Cardinal Primate. Soldiers and more bands.

"Oh, white walls of Spain!" Lorca once wrote; and from golden Toledo, we started south, making for these very walls in the unchanging *pueblos blancos* of Andalusia. Marchena, Osuna, Ronda. This land not only abounds in donkeys (still called *el vecino*, or one of the householders, in some districts), but it is also where the fighting bulls graze.

There are now more than a hundred bull-rearing ranches on the great estates of Andalusia, where the bulls are selected with great care, measured for their speed and valour. The ranch of Don Alvaro Domecq is undoubtedly one of the finest.

The Domecqs are fond of saying they live to celebrate the three traditional joys of Andalusia: wine, bulls, and horses. The sherry they produce in Jerez de la Frontera and its environs has dominated the British market for more than a century, even as the Domecqs have dominated Jerez itself for even longer. Indeed, say "La Familia" in Jerez de la Frontera, throughout Andalusia for that matter, and you can mean only one thing: the Domecq family. The present head of the family and the company, the largest producers of sherry and brandy in the world, is the tall, elegant José Ignacio Domecq, sometimes known as "The Nose" for his unrivalled ability to sniff out the excellence or defects in a blend.

As sherry is a blended wine, it therefore has no vintage years, everything depending on a house's method of sunning, crushing, fermenting, and maturing in casks. Jerez, with port facilities available in neighbouring Cadiz, is the sherry capital of Spain; the apex of a rich triangular chunk of Andalusia that includes two other sherry-producing towns, Sanlúcar de Barrameda, at the mouth of the Guadalquivir, and Puerto de Santa María. Between them, each year these three towns squeeze something like 15 million litres of golden wine out of their 20,000 chalky acres of vineyards.

The name sherry, from the archiac English spelling of the town's name, Xeres, was first used in England in 1608. Before that, at the court of Queen Elizabeth, it was called "sack," from the Spanish verb *"sacar,"* which means "to export."

Wine, bulls, horses.

Don Alvaro Domecq also runs a Spanish Riding School and takes his horses on international tours. In May, during the famous Feria del Caballo in Jerez, the town is gripped by two weeks of horse fever. There are races and other competitions, but, above all, there is an endless flow of sherry and flamenco in the *casetas*, which run the gamut from slapdash booth to elaborate, handsomely appointed pavilion, set up by the local clubs and sherry firms to entertain their friends, mostly by plying them with drink and song into the small hours, denying them any sleep whatsoever if possible. Without warning the croak of the flamenco singer is heard and, all at once, everybody in the seething pavilion is dancing, clapping, and shouting *olés*.

Flamenco is the cry of the true soul of Andalusia.

"As a people," Roger Fry has written, "the Spaniards have rarely attained to much intellectual, or for that matter esthetic, detachment — they have always accepted avidly the instinctive life, and yet their innate sense of logical clarity of proportion and design is so strong that even while they are being deliberately melodramatic, or abandoning themselves to the unrestrained expression of the fiercer emotions of life, they cannot forget altogether the claims of style.

"This same peculiar quality comes out I think no less in the flamenco songs. The peculiarity of these is that they are at once nearer to the *cri du coeur* than any music of passion or pathos, and yet they have nothing of the sentimentality that awaits such abandonment to emotion in the Northern races. They are at once intensely physiological and rigidly stylistic."

If today the most polished *tablaos* of flamenco can undoubtedly be seen in the nightclubs of Madrid, Malaga or Seville, it must be said that the music is at its most moving when it is not sought out, but catches you by surprise, on street corners or sleazy bars in the heat of a fiesta.

I heard my first flamenco, quite by accident, in a crowded sailors' bar not far from the Valencia waterfront, during the *Fallas* of 1952. Suddenly, magically, a grizzly old man produced a beat-up guitar, his leathery hands rippling over the strings and beating on the hardwood with an astonishing agility, and just as swiftly and unexpected a whore disentangled herself from somebody's embrace and leaped up on to the bar itself, lifting her skirts and beginning to dance. Soon everybody was singing and clapping, a drunken fisherman vaulting on to the bar to join the frenzied girl, sweat literally flying from them.

> *¡Fuego! ¡Fuego! ¡Fuego!*
> *Mundos y planetas en revolución*
> *con el fuego de me corazón!*

The Spaniard's obsession with death is manifest not only in the ritual of the bullfight, but also in the procession of the sixty brotherhoods during Semana Santa in Seville, of which Lorca wrote,

> *Por la calleja vienen*
> *extraños unicornios.*
> *¿De que campo,*

de qué bosque mitológico?
Más cerca,
ya parecen astrónomos,
fantásticos Merlines...

Down narrow streets they come,
strange unicorns.
From what fields,
from what forest of myth?
Nearer,
now they seem astronomers,
phantastical Merlins...

In the Good Friday procession in Seville the participants wear black or white or scarlet pointed hats, hoods and cloaks, only their eyes revealed; they carry long lighted candles; oboes and clarinets playing the "Whistlers of Silence." Each procession is comprised of a *cofradía,* a brotherhood whose membership is passed down from father to son. About forty float-bearers sweat under the burden of a *paso,* an enormous litter on which a pious wooden statue is mounted, bejewelled and garlanded with flowers. Each statue of Christ or the Virgin weighs something like seven tonnes. The float of *Cristo de la Buena Muerte* is traditionally carried by Spanish Foreign Legionnaires, singing their battle hymn, "I am the fiancé of Death." The more penitent march with heavy chains clamped to their feet and lug crosses barefoot. Spectators strew white carnations at their bloody footprints.

Immediately following Semana Santa, there is an outburst of joy, the April feria.

"There is nothing like it in our contemporary world," Sacheverell Sitwell wrote in 1950, "no such scene of popular and spontaneous enjoyment. Music as an art of pleasure and excitement plays here, night and day, unspoiled. Beautiful costumes in the Gypsy idiom give sparkle and colour and the illusion of crinolines, but without the whalebone cages. The young women on horseback and their cavaliers form a spectacle without equal as they ride slowly round and round the Feria in the midday heat. To drive among them in a mule carriage while the sidewalks are crowded with Sevillanas in their spotted crinolines is an excitement that is nearly indescribable; then, late in the afternoon, comes that extraordinary moment when from all over Seville, in every direction, you hear the rattle and crackle of castanets. The crowd is making for the Feria and the women are playing their castanets idly, and in anticipation, as they walk along.

"Soon they are dancing the *seguidilla* in a hundred different booths at once. All the lights of the fair go on at one and the same time. The fountains change colour. Under the electric lights the crowd is thicker than ever and moves up and down, watching the dancing, to the crackling of its own castanets, which breaks the rhythm; and young girls are dancing in little groups on the sidewalks. Round midnight the entire Feria is alive with music. Till three o'clock, or after, the dancing is general. It is a marvelous and never-to-be-forgotten feast of sight and sound. As you walk home and look back for the last time, leaving the lights and music behind you, your breath will be caught with the orange blossom, and falling asleep, forgetful of the hour, you may think, as I do, that the Feria of Seville must be the most beautiful public spectacle in the world today."

Once, Spain had fascinated me. Now, twenty-five years later, though I was hardly the same person, I still found it compelling. It's not a country, it's a time-machine. Cross the Pyrenees and you are at once not only in another culture, but adrift in a different era. In a land where, as Gerald Brenan once observed, the bald are more bald, the obese more obese, the thin more cadaverous, the one-legged more limbless than in other countries.

It is a land of cathedrals both ornate and arrogant.

In Salamanca, Toledo, Burgos and Barcelona. The Barcelona of Gaudi's never to be completed Church of the Holy Family.

Or in Seville, where we wandered footsore through a cathedral of incredible flamboyance. The building was begun in 1401, over the ruins of a mosque, after it was declared: "Let us build a cathedral so immense that everyone on beholding it will take us for madmen."

It is also the country of incomparable Granada.

"Life holds no greater sadness, none, than to be blind in Granada."

In 1492, at a point on the Motril road to the south of Granada, a point called Suspiro del Moro – The Moor's Sigh – the last Moorish king, Abu 'Abdu'llah, paused to weep for the city he had lost. His mother, obviously a honey, is said to have turned on him: "You weep like a woman for what you could not hold as a man." After 781 years the Moorish domination of Spain had ended.

Its legacy, everyone's legacy, is the exquisite Alhambra, built by the Nasrim princes. Though the conquering Christians vandalized the place – wall hangings and carpets pilfered, the furniture gone – the remaining sculpture on the walls and ceilings was something I could only marvel at. So, for that matter, were the modelled pillars, the proportions of the various chambers and galleries and gardens, the vistas from the balconies, and indeed the very layout of the Alhambra. In the Hall of the Ambassadors, the audience chamber of the Moorish kings, for instance, more than 150 patterns and inscriptions from the Koran have been impressed into the pillar and ceiling decorations. In the Abencerrajes Gallery, bloody history intrudes. Here the father of Boabdil, Mulay Abu'l Hasan, had all the sons of his first wife decapitated, their heads flung into a central basin, in order to secure succession for the son of his second wife.

Then there's Córdoba.

Córdoba, like so many things in Spain, caught us by surprise. We came upon the city after a seemingly endless drive through bone-dry La Mancha, its fields sown with saffron and cereal. Suddenly we were out of the tableland, rising into craggy mountain corridors, the road twisting through hills thick with olive trees, and there, to astonish us, was Córdoba.

Córdoba, where the Emirs from the Damascus Caliphate established themselves as early as 719, building a mosque, a forest of pillars, the arches extending apparently endlessly in all directions. Córdoba, where Columbus finally obtained Queen Isabella's commission for his voyage of discovery.

"And your Highnesses have ordered that I should go, not by land, towards the East, which is the accustomed route, but by the way of the West, whereby hitherto nobody to our knowledge has ever been. And so, after having expelled all the Jews from all your kingdoms and lordships, in this same month of January, Your Highnesses ordered me to set out, with a sufficient fleet, for the said country of India, to this end, Your Highnesses have shown me great favour..."

The topography of Spain is incredibly varied, and the language can differ from province to province.

The Basques, endowed by Adam, speak the language of angels, and in thrusting Catalonia, the industrial heart of the country, they speak Catalan. Why, even tiny Ibiza, third largest of the Balearic Islands, has its own tongue: Ibicenco.

But, for all that, there is a shared Iberian attitude, a grace that informs all of Spain. Grace, and a measure of madness, that has endeared the country to me beyond any other in Europe.

Only in Spain, for instance, can anarchy be adjudged not a sentimental notion, but rather a mainstream cause with serious political ambitions.

Only in Pamplona do young men risk their lives once a year for the hell of it. Just to show off. Early each morning, during the Fiesta of San Fermín, there is an *encierro*, an early morning bull run. The bulls are released from pens to run through the palisaded streets to the Plaza de Toros. Young men, armed only with rolled up newspapers, race ahead of them. Some are gored, others are trampled by the charging bulls.

In Spain, flagellants still march in some religious processions.

The Spanish peasant, as Hemingway once observed, knows death is the unescapable reality, the one thing any man can be sure of: "...and when they have a religion they have one which believes that life is shorter than death."

Look at it this way.

In this age of computers and ill-manners, such is the profound courtesy of the fife and drum band in the Semana Santa procession in Seville that it will pause in its playing if a singer, any singer, in the crowd raises his or her voice in a *saeta,* an improvised religious lament, a variant of flamenco.

Like you, I can readily summon up a list of countries with a better standard of living, less violence raw or ritualized, but none where I would rather wander footloose, taking my chances with strangers.

Such is the Spaniard's awareness of death that his dignity, his appetite for life, his ability to seize the day, has no equal in my experience.

It is a country to be celebrated.

I beria is like a bull's hide, extending in length from west to east, its fore parts toward the east, and in breadth from north to south....This is the most westerly point, not only of Europe, but of the whole inhabited world.

STRABO, *GEOGRAPHY,* C. 29-27 B.C.

Spain! It hangs like a drying ox hide outside the southern door of Europe proper. Some have seen in its outlines the head of a knight encased in armour, the top of his casque in the Pyrenees, the tip of his chin at Portugal's Cabo de São Vicente, his nose at Lisboa, his iron-girt eyes looking westward across the Atlantic. I see Spain as a kaleidoscope of high, sun-baked plateaus, snow-crowned mountains and swamps of the Guadalquivir. No one of these images takes precedence over the other, for I have known fine days in each of these three contrasting terrains.

JAMES A. MICHENER, *IBERIA,* 1968

A Continent Unto Itself

37 The Cantabrian Coast, north of Bilbao. An oasis. Stretching from the Pyrenees to Cape Finisterre along the Bay of Biscay and inland to the Cantabrian Cordillera, this verdant country enjoys the wettest climate in a parched land. Because of the blessed abundance of rain, the farmhouses here are scattered rather than clustered around a single source of water, as they are in most of Spain.

The road from Pamplona to Roncesvalles is twenty-eight miles of Switzerland; there are cow-bells and chalets, green meadows and wild roses, pine trees, and white tufts of water that come tumbling down perpendicular rock faces through clumps of maidenhair fern. And the stolid Basques upon this road would as soon pay customs duty as click a pair of castanets. Indeed, I thought, a visit to Granada must be as great a change to the people of Navarre as Naples to an Aberdonian.

H. V. MORTON, *A STRANGER IN SPAIN*, 1955

39 The Aragón Valley. Dry Spain begins. Separated from the north by the Pyrenees (top of photo) and the Cantabrian Cordillera to the west, this desiccated valley is largely without rain.

40 Rugged La Calobra on the northwest coast of Majorca is in startling contrast to the rest of the island, which is very flat. A road, one of Spanish engineering's zanier triumphs, twists tortuously down to the sea through a bleak moonscape of jagged peaks.

41 The Picos de Europa. These limestone mountains, the heart of the highest range in the Cantabrian Cordillera, confront the Atlantic and proffer an almost impenetrable barrier to communications with Castile in the south. The Picos de Europa were the last refuge of the Christians after the Arab invasion of 711, and they also won their first victory here, under the leadership of Pelayo (c. 722), who began the reconquest. Herds of wild horses still roam these mountain pastures.

God does not count the number of spear heads, but gives the palm of victory to whomever he chooses. The small army of the Christians left their cave in the mountain to fight the Moors, who, as they began to retreat, were divided into two groups. Alqama, their leader, was killed right there, and the traitor Bishop Oppas was taken prisoner. In that place one hundred and twenty-five thousand Moors died. The other sixty-three thousand climbed to the very top of mount Aseuva and descended to Liebana through Amuesa. But not even these escaped the Lord's vengeance. As they were crossing over the mountain on the borders of the Deva River, in the district of Cosgaya, the mountain, unfastening its foundations, hurled the sixty-three thousand into the river and crushed all of them. Even today, when the river-bed can be seen, there appear many signs of these men.

CHRISTIAN CHRONICLE, c. 880

42 A tableland of barren hills between Benahadux and Tabernas, north of Almeria.

The site of Almería was surrounded everywhere by mounds of bare rocks, hard and angular, with no top soil. It would seem that a stony waste had been chosen for its site and the land stripped of its dust with a sieve.

AL-IDRISI (ARABIC GEOGRAPHER), 1147

The sun beat down and it was as if the stony ground had stored up heat from yesterday's sun and was now releasing it into the already too warm air. Farms lay solitary, endlessly far from each other, their fortress-like walls a protection against wild beasts and wicked men. Not a tree was in sight and the only green touch was in some big cacti whose spongy leaves swelled up like fungi in rock crevices or behind fallen walls. Heavily laden wagons drawn by six or eight mules gave some life to the otherwise dead, burnt desert. It was as though a devouring flood had covered the whole landscape, as though the burning air had consumed every blade of grass and left not even the ash thereof behind.

HANS CHRISTIAN ANDERSEN, *A VISIT TO SPAIN,* 1862

43 *The grasslands west of Pamplona. The lush grasslands of Navarre, the province of transition between "wet" and "dry" Spain. Fields and streams are lined with beech and poplars.*

The scenery is alpine and picturesque. The trout fishing and wild shooting excellent, the valleys are beautiful, especially those of Bastán (meaning "garden" in Arabic), Santiesteban and Cincovillas....The highlanders of Navarre are remarkable for their light active physical forms, their temperate habits, endurance of hardships and privation, individual bravery, and love of perilous adventure; the pursuits of the chase, smuggling, and a dash of robbery, form their moral education: thus their sinewy limbs are braced, and their hawk-eyed self-reliance sharpened.

RICHARD FORD, *HANDBOOK FOR SPAIN,* 1845

45 *The plateau of Extremadura, dry Extremadura, where only cork trees, grazing sheep, and* conquistadores *seem to thrive. Cortés, Pizarro, Balboa, and de Soto quit this hard land to find glory and wealth across the seas.*

After lunch, as it was still too hot for walking, we took a taxi to visit the so-called Lake of Proserpine, which is a Roman reservoir lying some three miles outside the town [Merida]. Mounting a low rise, we came suddenly upon a wide stretch of undulating country, covered with rocks, grass, asphodels and a few scattered ilex trees. This is the beginning of the great sheep and cattle-raising region of Extremadura that stretches northward to Salamanca and west to Portugal. Below, in a hollow, lay a blue lake, some half a mile in diameter. So clear, so blue it looked among its rocky margins that one would have said it was a lough in County Clare or Connemara.

GERALD BRENAN, *THE FACE OF SPAIN,* 1951

47 *San Sebastián, celebrated as the "Pearl" of the Cantabrian Coast, is the leading summer resort in the country. It is also the official summer seat of the Spanish government.*

Even on a hot day San Sebastían has a certain early-morning quality. The trees seem as though their leaves were never quite dry. The streets feel as though they had just been sprinkled. It is always cool and shady on certain streets on the hottest day.

ERNEST HEMINGWAY, *THE SUN ALSO RISES,* 1926

48 *Sand dunes at Coto Doñana National Park, on the southwest coast. Today, a wildlife sanctuary, it was once a hunting preserve for nobility.*

This fertile district was called the garden of Hercules, and was reserved by [king] St. Ferdinand as the lion's share at the capture of Seville [from the Moors in 1248]. It produced the finest Baetican olives of antiquity: under the Moors it was a paradise, but now all is ruin and desolation. The Spaniards and their *talas* [felling of trees] ravaged everything, and broken roads and bridges mark their former warfare...meanwhile there is not only excellent lodging for owls in ruined buildings, but first-rate cover for game of every kind, which thrive in these wastes. No man who is fond of shooting will fail spending a week either at the Coto del Rey or at that of Doñana.

RICHARD FORD, *HANDBOOK FOR SPAIN,* 1845

49 *The erosion of these sandstone formations along the Costa Blanca, which runs north and south of Alicante, has created the vast sandy beaches for which the area is famous. Once Greek settlements thrived here, now bikinis are the rule, the golden rule.*

One of the pleasures of living in Spain is the enlarged sense one gets of the passage of time. In England the day is broken up by a thousand little fences and obstacles, which produce a feeling of frustration and worry. One passes from breakfast to supper with struggle and effort, and when night comes one feels one has not had a day at all. Nothing of interest has happened, no taste or color has been left to mark out that day from all others. But in Spain time imitates the landscape. It is vast, untrammeled, featureless and every day gives the sensation of a week.

GERALD BRENAN, *THE FACE OF SPAIN,* 1951

51 *Sheep graze in Andalusia, the southernmost region of Spain. The rolling foothills of the Sierra Nevada are mild in winter, hot and dry in summer. Andalusia is not only sheep-grazing country, but also the home of the bravest bulls and the greatest bullfighters: Belmonte, Joselito, Manolete.*

Whichever way you approach Andalusia, you must cross mountains and descend into the fairest and most fertile region of Spain. The road began to rise towards the mighty flanks of the Sierra Morena and to twist and turn, so that at one moment the sun was in my eyes and the next at my back. This country used to be frequented by bandits a century ago and men would make their wills before venturing into it, as they did in the eighteenth century before they entered the Highlands of Scotland. It is said that a few Reds still lurk about the *sierra,* in whose less accessible parts you may remember that Don Quixote underwent his penance.

H. V. MORTON, *STRANGER IN SPAIN,* 1955

52 *The palm grove at Elche, one of the most extensive in Europe, contains more than one hundred thousand trees. Although it dates from the Roman period, the forest was developed by the Arabs.*

A palm tree I beheld in Ar-Rusāfa,
Far in the West, far from the palm-tree land;
I said: You, like myself, are far away, in a strange land;
How long have I been far away from my people!
You grew up in a land where you are a stranger,
And, like myself, are living in the farthest corner of the earth:
May the morning clouds refresh you at this distance,
And may abundant rains comfort you forever!

'ABD AR-RAHMĀN AD-DĀHIL,
(AN EMIGRÉ IN SPAIN, FROM DAMASCUS), 756-788

Man is here the vigorous plant of a strong soil; here he stands erect, full of personal dignity and individual worth and independence.

RICHARD FORD, *HANDBOOK FOR SPAIN, 1845*

As we move about we look at the passing faces, so lovely or so deeply marked – either preternaturally solemn with the leaden solemnity of Spaniards or else more than usually gay and animated. The bald are more bald, the obese more obese, the thin more cadaverous, the one-legged more limbless than in other countries.

GERALD BRENAN, *THE FACE OF SPAIN,* 1951

The Faces of Spain

57 *A shepherd in Marquiz de Alba, Zamora, wearing the traditional cloak, rarely seen in Spain today. He is in the fields twenty-four hours a day, seven days a week. When asked if he was ever lonely and to whom he talked, the shepherd pointed to his two thousand sheep and said, "I talk to my friends."*

Ya se van los pastores	The shepherds are going away
a la Extremadura;	to Extremadura;
ya se queda la sierra	the Sierra is now left
triste y oscura.	sad and deserted.

SPANISH FOLKSONG

58 *A farmer with his donkey, at Chodes, Zaragoza. The old saddle is made of straw and wood.*

As they were proceeding in this manner, they saw coming down the road toward them a man mounted upon an ass, who, as he drew near, appeared to them to be a gypsy. But Sancho Panza, whose heart and soul were stirred every time he caught sight of a donkey, had no sooner laid eyes on the fellow than he recognized him as Ginés de Pasamonte, and in this case the gypsy served as the thread that led him to the yarn-ball of his stolen gray, for it was indeed the gray upon which Pasamonte was riding. That worthy, in order to dispose of the ass and avoid being identified, had got himself up in gypsy costume, for he knew how to speak their language and many others as if they had been his native tongue.

As soon as Sancho had seen and recognized him, he called out at the top of his voice, "Hey, Ginesillo, you thief! Release my jewel, my treasure, my life, the beast on which I take my rest. Flee, you whoring knave; begone, you robber, and leave me that which is not yours!"

All these words and insults were quite unnecessary, for at the first sound of Sancho's voice Ginés had leaped down and, trotting, or, better, running, away, had soon left them all behind. Sancho then went up to the gray and threw his arms around it.

"How have you been, old friend," he said, " joy of my life, apple of my eye?" With this, he kissed and caressed it as if it had been a person, the ass standing quietly all the while, submitting without a word to this show of affection.

CERVANTES, *DON QUIXOTE,* 1615

59 *Men clipping mules in Sepúlveda, Segovia.*

The mules in Spain, as in the East, have their coats closely shorn or clipped; part of the hair is usually left on in stripes like the zebra, or cut into fanciful patterns, like the tattooings of an Indian chief. This process of shearing is found to keep the beast cooler and freer from cutaneous disorders. The operation is performed in the southern provinces by gipsies, *"gitanos,"* who are the same tinkers, horse-dealers, and vagrants in Spain as elsewhere. In the northern provinces all this is done by Arragonese, who, in costume, good-for-nothingness, and most respects, are no better than the worst real gipsies.

The mule-clippers are called *"esquiladores":* they may be known by the formidable shears...which they carry in their sashes. They are very particular in clipping the pastern and heels, which they say ought to be as free from hair as the palm of a lady's hand.

RICHARD FORD, *HANDBOOK FOR SPAIN, 1845*

60 In the Rastro, or Flea Market, in Madrid, a man sells handmade canes.

61 Old men talking over a game of cards in Casares, Málaga.

God wanted that men should have naturally all kinds of enjoyment, so that they could face sorrows and difficulties when they befell. For this reason men decided to search for ways in which they could obtain such joy plentifully. Hence they discovered and made up many games and forms of entertainment, to enjoy themselves. Some of the games are played on horseback,...others on foot,...others sitting down, such as chess, checkers, dice and many others. Sitting-down games are the most common, since they can be played night or day, by women who do not ride and stay at home, and by men when they grow old and weak.

ALFONSO X, KING OF CASTILE (1254-82), *THE BOOK OF CHESS*

62 At ten every morning in Torneros, León, a woman walks through the village. As she passes each door, the people let their goats out. By the time she reaches the end of the village, a cloud of dust fills the air. In the evening she retraces her route, and all the goats return to their homes.

The soil of the Central Plateau is a very poor one—*dura tellus Iberia* [the harsh land of Iberia], as Pliny calls it—and except in certain favoured spots it requires great industry to make a living by cultivating it. So uncertain is the rainfall that crop failures and their attendant famines are frequent. Often it is only by practising a kind of village communism that the peasants are able to get along at all. At the same time there are immense steppe lands ranged over by flocks and herds which at certain seasons become migratory....Now this is a type of society which is not confined to Spain, but appears whenever certain climatic conditions prevail. It is strongly developed in Persia and in North Africa....The famous orientalism of the Spaniards is not due to "Arab blood" but to climate and geography.

GERALD BRENAN, *THE SPANISH LABYRINTH,* 1943

63 This woman still works in the fields with her family at Mecina Alfahar, Granada. Behind her, a kid, still too young to roam loose, is tied with a piece of string.

The peasants of no country upon earth are more patient of heat, of hunger and of thirst, or capable of greater exertions than this very people who have been accused of indolence.

JOSEPH TOWNSEND, *JOURNEY THROUGH SPAIN,* 1787

64 A novice bullfighter in Belmonte, Cuenca, practises passes with an imaginary bull in an empty churchyard.

65 A matador in Madrid wears the traditional "suit of light." Usually of satin, these costumes are richly embroidered in gold, silver, or coloured silk.

66 Many of the little villages in Spain are self-sufficient and have their own sawmills. A man in Bercianos de Aliste, Zamora, feeds eucalyptus logs into a mill. Farmers cut timber on their land when they need it and take it to the village mills as they have for centuries.

67 In the famous Basque fishing village of Bermeo, Vizcaya, they build boats in the old manner, out of wood, using an adze to form the frame, then hammering on hull planking with galvanized spikes.

From the first Spanish discoveries in America till the time of our own New England clipper ships, the Basque coast was the backbone of Spanish trade. The three provinces were the only ones which kept their privileges and their municipal liberties all through the process of the centralizing of the Spanish monarchy with cross and faggot, which historians call the great period of Spain. The rocky inlets in the mountains were full of shipyards that turned out privateers and merchantmen manned by lanky broad-shouldered men with hard red-beaked faces and huge hands coarsened by generations of straining on heavy oars and halyards–men who feared only God and the sea-spirits of their strange mythology and were a law unto themselves, adventurers and bigots.

JOHN DOS PASSOS, *ROSINANTE TO THE ROAD AGAIN*, 1922

68 Nuns in Atocha Station, Madrid.

69 The cathedral at Tarragona.

There is no doubt that the Spanish people are profoundly religious. Their inherent religion, moreover, harmonizes in many points with the Catholic faith. The synthetic and spontaneous nature of Spanish thought, for instance, is readily attracted by the doctrine of a revealed dogma, and there are obvious lines of sympathy between the transcendental pessimism of the Catholic and the experimental pessimism of the stoic–stoicism being at bottom the natural attitude of the Spanish soul. Such an attitude places the subject in the mood of a contemplative spectator who sees the world as drama, a point again on which the stoic Spaniard can find himself at home in the Roman faith. Add the Spanish tendency to lay stress on synthetic human standards rather than on ethical values, and we shall see how deeply the Catholic roots have struck ready earth in the Spanish race.

SALVADOR DE MADARIAGA, *SPAIN, A MODERN HISTORY*, 1942

70 A man in a horsecart, La Puebla, Ciudad Real.

71 A young man in the traditional Andalusian costume stops to aid an oxcart in the mud on the gypsy pilgrimage to El Rocío.

She was well matched by a brother, nearly about her own age; they were perfect models of the Andalusian *majo* and *maja*. He was tall, vigorous and well-formed, with a clear olive-complexion, a dark beaming eye and curling chestnut whiskers that met under his chin. He was gallantly dressed in a short green velvet jacket, fitted to his shape, profusely decorated with silver buttons, with a white handkerchief in each pocket. He had breeches of the same, with rows of buttons from the hips to the knees, a pink silk handkerchief round his neck, gathered through a ring, on the bosom of a neatly planted shirt, a sash round the waist to match, *botines* or spatterdashes of the finest russet-leather, elegantly worked and open at the calf to show his stocking, and russet-shoes, setting off a well-shaped foot.

WASHINGTON IRVING, *TALES OF THE ALHAMBRA*, 1832

72 Gypsy women begging in Cáceres, Cáceres.

In the greatest bullfight ever
At Ronda's ancient circus seen –
Five jet-black bulls, for their devices
Wearing rosettes of black and green!...
The girls turned up with shrilling voices
In painted gigs and jaunting-cars
Displaying their round fans embroidered
With sequins glittering like stars...
The lads of Ronda came in riding
Affected, supercilious mares,
With wide grey hats upon their eyebrows
Pulled slantwide down with rakish airs.
The tiers (all hats and towering combs)
Where people had begun to pack,
Round, like the zodiac, revolving,
Were pied with laughter white and black;
And when the mighty Cayetano
Strode over the straw-coloured sands
Dressed in his apple-coloured costume
Broidered with silk and silver bands,
From all the fighters in the ring
He stood so boldly out alone
Before the great black bulls of jet
Which Spain from her own earth had grown –
The afternoon went gipsy-coloured
Bronzing its tan to match his own.
If you had seen with what a grace
He moved his legs, and seemed to swim:
What equilibrium was his
With cape and swordcloth deft and trim:
Romero, torrying the stars
In heaven, could scarcely match with him!
He killed five bulls, five jet-black bulls
Wearing rosettes of black and green.
Upon the sharp point of his sword
Five flowers he opened to be seen.
Grazing the muzzles of the brutes,
Each instant you could see him glide,
Like a great butterfly of gold
With rosy wings fanned open wide.
The circus, with the afternoon
Vibrated, in the uproar swaying;
And in between the scent of blood
That of the mountain-tops went straying.

FEDERICO GARCÍA LORCA, *MARIANA PINEDA*, 1925

Festivals and Pageants

77 Originally a butchers' festival, the San Fermín or Running of the Bulls in Pamplona lasts for a week in July. At seven each morning, the bulls are released from their pens to begin their run through the streets to the bullring. Oxen (the white animals) are mixed in to keep the herd together. The bulls are not dangerous if they remain in a pack, but once isolated a single bull will charge anything that moves.

79 Ahead of the bulls run the sanfermines, the young men of Pamplona dressed in white shirts with red kerchiefs around their necks and wearing special slippers with rubber soles. They carry rolled newspapers as their only protection. If they fall they use the newspapers to distract the bulls.

81 In this dangerous stretch in front of the Military Hospital there are few places to find protection from the charging bulls.

83 Those who do not move fast enough are sometimes gored, but more often they are trampled by the bulls.

We landed at Pamplona at night. The streets were solid with people dancing. Music was pounding and throbbing. Fireworks were being set off from the big public square. All the carnivals I had ever seen paled down in comparison. A rocket exploded over our heads with a blinding burst and the stick came whirling and whishing down. Dancers, snapping their fingers and whirling in perfect time through the crowd, bumped into us before we could get our bags....We started off through the dark, narrow, carnival-mad streets with a boy carrying our rucksacks. It was a lovely big room in an old Spanish house with walls thick as a fortress. A cool, pleasant room, with a red tile floor and two big, comfortable beds set back in an alcove. A window opened on to an iron grilled porch out over the street. We were very comfortable.

All night long the wild music kept up in the street below. Several times in the night there was a wild roll of drumming, and I got out of bed and across the tiled floor to the balcony. But it was always the same. Men, blue-shirted, bareheaded, whirling and floating in a wild fantastic dance down the street behind the rolling drums and shrill fifes.

Just at daylight there was a crash of music in the street below. Real military music. Herself was up, dressed, at the window.

"Come on," she said. "They're all going somewhere." Down below the street was full of people. It was five o'clock in the morning. They were all going in one direction. I dressed in a hurry and we started after them.

The crowd was all going toward the great public square. People were pouring into it from every street and moving out of it toward the open country we could see through the narrow gaps in the high walls.

We started out after the crowd. Out of a narrow gate into a great yellow open space of country with the new concrete bull ring standing high and white and black with people. The yellow and red Spanish flag blowing in the early morning breeze. Across the open and once inside the bull ring, we mounted to the top looking toward the town. It cost a peseta to go up to the top. All the other levels were free. There were easily twenty thousand people there. Everyone jammed on the outside of the big concrete amphitheatre, looking toward the yellow town with the bright red roofs, where a long wooden pen ran from the entrance of the city gate across the open, bare ground to the bull ring.

It was really a double wooden fence, making a long entryway from the main street of the town into the bull ring itself. It made a runway about two hundred and fifty yards long. People were jammed solid on each side of it. Looking up it toward the main street.

Then far away there was a dull report.

"They're off," everybody shouted.

"What is it?" I asked a man next to me who was leaning far out over the concrete rail.

"The bulls! They have released them from the corrals on the far side of the city. They are racing through the city."

"Whew," said Herself. "What do they do that for?"

Then down the narrow fenced-in runway came a crowd of men and boys running. Running as hard as they could go. The gate feeding into the bull ring was opened and they all ran pell-mell under the entrance levels into the ring. Then there came another crowd. Running even harder. Straight up the long pen from the town.

"Where are the bulls?" asked Herself.

Then they came in sight. Eight bulls galloping along, full tilt, heavy set, black, glistening, sinister, their horns bare, tossing their heads. And running with them three steers with bells on their necks. They ran in a solid mass, and ahead of them sprinted, tore, ran and bolted the rear guard of the men and boys of Pamplona who had allowed themselves to be chased through the streets for a morning's pleasure.

A boy in his blue shirt, red sash, white canvas shoes with the inevitable leather wine bottle hung from his shoulders stumbled as he sprinted down the straightaway. The first bull lowered his head and made a jerky, sideways toss. The boy crashed up against the fence and lay there limp, the herd running solidly together passed him up. The crowd roared.

Everybody made a dash for the inside of the ring, and we got into a box just in time to see the bulls come into the ring filled with men. The men ran in a panic to each side. The bulls, still bunched solidly together, ran straight with the trained steers across the ring and into the entrance that led to the pens.

That was the entry. Every morning during the bull fighting festival of San Fermín at Pamplona the bulls that are to fight in the afternoon are released from their corrals at six o'clock in the morning and race through the main street of the town for a mile and a half to the pen. The men who run ahead of them do it for the fun of the thing. It has been going on each year since a couple of hundred years before Columbus had his historic interview with Queen Isabella in the camp outside of Granada.

There are two things in favour of there being no accidents. First, that fighting bulls are not aroused and vicious when they are together. Second, that the steers are relied upon to keep them moving.

Sometimes things go wrong, a bull will be detached from the herd as they pile through into the pen and with his crest up, a ton of speed and viciousness, his needle-sharp horns lowered, will charge again and again into the packed mass of men and boys in the bull ring. There is no place for the men to get out of the ring. It is too jammed for them to climb over the barrera or red fence that rims the field. They have to stay in and take it. Eventually the steers get the bull out of the ring and into the pen. He may wound or kill thirty men before they can get him out. No armed men are allowed to oppose him. That is the chance the Pamplona bull fight fans take every morning during the Feria. It is the Pamplona tradition of giving the bulls a final shot at everyone in town before they enter the pens. They will not leave until they come out into the glare of the arena to die in the afternoon.

ERNEST HEMINGWAY, *THE TORONTO STAR WEEKLY*, 1923

86 The Corpus Christi Procession in Toledo is held on the second Thursday after Pentecost. The silver-gilt monstrance dates from the sixteenth century. The gold of the custodial at its centre was brought from America by Columbus.

87 The solemn Corpus Christi Procession winds through the city's ancient and twisting streets following a tapestry hung above the route. Richly embroidered in the vicinity of the cathedral, the tapestry is worn and patched in those areas farthest along the route.

I should now tell you that I have seen the ceremony on Corpus Christi Day, which is very solemnly kept here. There's a general procession of all the parishes and monasteries, which are very numerous. The streets through which the Holy Sacrament is to pass are hung with the richest tapestry in the world; for I do not only speak of that which belongs to the Crown...but also of that which belongs to a thousand particular persons which have most admirable tapestry. All the balconies are then without their lattices, adorned with carpets, rich cushions, and canopies. They hang ticking across the streets to hinder the sun from being troublesome, and they throw water upon it to make the air cooler. All the streets are spread with sand, well watered, and filled with so great quantity of flowers that one can hardly tread upon anything else. The Repositories are extraordinarily large, and adorned with the greatest splendour.

The whole Court without exception followed the Holy Sacrament; the Councils walked after it without any order or precedence, as they happened to be, holding white wax candles in their hands; the King had one and went foremost, next the tabernacle where the Sacrament was. It is certainly one of finest ceremonies that can be seen. I observed that all the gentlemen of the Bed-chamber had a great gold key by their sides. It opens the King's chamber, into which they can go when they will; it is as big as a cellar-door key. I there saw several Knights of Malta, who wore every one a cross of Malta, made of holland, and embroidered upon their cloaks. It was near two o'clock and the procession was not yet gone in; when it passed by the palace they fired several rockets and other inventions.

MADAME D'AULNOY, *TRAVELS INTO SPAIN*, 1691

89 One of the Moor and Christian Festivals traditionally held in the Spanish Levant, this
91 one took place in Onteniente, in the province of Valencia. From 711 to 1492 the tenacious Moors occupied at least some portion of the Iberian Peninsula. The long process of the Christian reconquest, and its triumphs, are still celebrated every summer in the southwestern part of the country. Battles that took place during the eight-hundred-year struggle are re-created, the locals dressing up in outlandish costumes, caricaturing the dress of the Moors, Berbers, and Christians. Even when the battle, the noisier the better, lasts for as long as six hours, it is a case of art improving on imperfect history, the Christians always emerging victorious.

Alone upon the battle ground, beneath a dying star,
Rodrigo stood in bleak despair, his host were scattered far;
Eight battles had they bravely fought against the Moorish band,
No hope remained within their hearts to save their native land.

BALLAD, TRANSLATED BY KATHARINE E. STRATHDEE

92 The captain of the Christian army arrives to claim his victory over the Moors.

As a people the Spaniards have rarely attained to much intellectual, or for that matter esthetic, detachment – they have always accepted avidly the instinctive life, and yet their innate sense of logical clarity of proportion and design is so strong that even while they are being deliberately melodramatic, or abandoning themselves to the unrestrained expression of the fiercer emotions of life, they cannot forget altogether the claims of style.

This same peculiar quality comes out I think no less in the Flamenco songs. The peculiarity of these is that they are at once nearer to the *cri du coeur* than any other music of passion or pathos, and yet they have nothing of the sentimentality that awaits such abandonment to emotion in the Northern races. They are at once intensely physiological and rigidly stylistic.

ROGER FRY, *A SAMPLER OF CASTILLE,* 1923

The Lights of the Fair

97 *A couple pauses for a glass of sherry at the April Fair in Seville. Beginning the Tuesday*
99 *after Easter Week, and lasting six days, the feria originated as a cattle fair in the nineteenth century. Today it is one of the most colourful festivals in Europe. People on horseback or riding in carriages parade along a roadway hung with Chinese lanterns. Brightly striped tents line the sides, offering refreshments. The participants in the festival wear the traditional local costume: for the men, a white shirt, short black or grey jacket, and red cummerbund and chaps; for the women, a full skirt, usually with a polka-dot design.*

If any one can be found to question the beauty of Spanish women, he should go to the Feria at Seville. This is especially a woman's festival, and the beautiful women of Andalusia, and, indeed, of Spain generally, crowd to Seville for the three days during which it is held. If the foreign visitor to the Prado de San Sebastian at this time has ever before in his life anywhere seen so many beautiful women beautifully dressed he may count himself happy. The national costumes of Spain may be dying out, but on such an occasion as this the shawl and the mantilla are universal, and in Seville, at all events, the Andalusian woman betrays little desire to seek for new fashions from Paris....

She wears a shawl, as, indeed, all Spanish women do, but the Sevillian woman is distinguished by the manner of wearing it; she folds it in oblong, not triangular, shape, so that it lies straight across the back and hangs over each arm; this method requires a little more skill than the triangular method, but, so worn, the shawl becomes a more expressive garment and adds a distinction to the wearer. The Feria is a marvellous display of beautiful and various shawls—which are often, even when belonging to the poor, very costly—and they are nearly always worn in this way. There are, indeed, exceptions to this rule; some of the small and more elaborate Manila shawls cannot thus be worn, and the old women also wear the shawl cross-wise with a point hanging down, and at the same time do their hair at the back and not at the top of the head. The peculiar erection of the hair at the top of the head, the flowers that adorn it, and the method of wearing the shawl are a kind of coquettish war-paint, the appanage of youth and vigour.

HAVELOCK ELLIS, *THE SOUL OF SPAIN*, 1908

101 *These people are members of two of the more than fifty religious confraternities that take*
102 *part in the Holy Week processions in Seville. Every day from Palm Sunday to Easter Saturday, these processions leave the church where the brotherhood originates and wind their way through the streets of the town to the cathedral and then return to their home church. As well as the members of the confraternity who march in their distinctive robes, the processions usually include two floats, or pasos, one with a statue of Jesus Christ and the other of the Virgin Mary.*

It is night...about ten o'clock....The star-studded sky seems to have dropped very low, to be resting indeed, on the figure of Faith standing motionless on the top of the Giralda. From a curve in the road near the Cathedral, a double line of lights is approaching, tiny sparks which presently prove to be huge candles. They are carried by figures completely hidden under robes of scarlet, brown, purple or white. A tall peaked cap with a mask over the face conceals every feature except the eyes....Mounted Roman Soldiers, companies of buglers and shrouded men with drums vary the monotonous stream of candle-bearers, among whom, here and there, you may see a pair of bare and blistered feet; and in smaller places where the pious spectacle has not been exploited, where a simpler and more devout spirit animates the procession, you will not infrequently see some penitent dragging a heavy chain along the line of march, or refusing to ease his task by accepting a sip of water.

"She comes!"

A hush falls over the crowd, members of which try to clear sufficient space to drop to their knees. A dazzling image of the Virgin, life sized, seated on an enormous platform of silver, ablaze with a hundred candles, is carried on the shoulders of men hidden beneath heavy folds of brocade or velvet.

MADGE MACBETH, *OVER THE GANGPLANK TO SPAIN*, 1931

103 *As is common in the north of Spain, the Holy Week observances at Bercianos de Aliste, Zamora, are much more sombre and less colourful than those in the south.*

105 *On Good Friday at Bercianos de Aliste, the members of the brotherhoods wear sombre attire for their devotions. The emphasis is on penitence.*

106 *The children's procession in Zamora on Palm Sunday.*

In Castile the peasant has nothing of the simple-mindedness, combined as always with cunning, of the Catalan or Gallego. He lives in a country with as severe a climate as any that is farmed, but it is a very healthy country; he has food, wine, his wife and children, or he has had them, but he has no comfort, nor much capital and these possessions are not ends in themselves; they are only a part of life and life is something that comes before death. Some one with English blood has written: "Life is real; life is earnest, and the grave is not its goal." And where did they bury him? and what became of the reality and the earnestness? The people of Castile have great common sense. They could not produce a poet who would write a line like that. They know death is the unescapable reality, the one thing any man may be sure of; the only security; that it transcends all modern comforts and that with it you do not need a bathtub in every American home, nor, when you have it, do you need the radio. They think a great deal about death and when they have a religion they have one which believes that life is much shorter than death.

ERNEST HEMINGWAY, 1931-2

107 *Gypsy oxcarts on pilgrimage to El Rocío from Seville. The Shrine of El Rocío was*
109 *built to celebrate the discovery of a statue of the Virgin Mary that had been hidden*
111 *there during the Moorish Conquest. Only two of the brotherhoods, from the gypsy suburbs of Seville, still use oxcarts on the yearly pilgrimage to El Rocío at Pentecost, the others now favouring tractors. The gypsies travel along back roads that cross the large estates, fording rivers and camping out each night during the four-day journey. Remarkably, the town of El Rocío is occupied only for the few days of the festival, families and* cofradias *maintaining houses there just for use during the pilgrimage. The festival, mind you, is attended not only by the gypsies of Seville, but by many of the faithful throughout Andalusia, maybe 100,000 strong.*

The Romeria del Rocío, like the Feria, is one of the most beautiful survivals into this "utility," "dehydrated" age. It sets forth from Seville at Whitsun, and is to be seen making its way through the Gypsy suburb of Triana. The procession consists of a number of high, two-wheeled waggons drawn by pairs of oxen. First, a waggon which is a moving or nomad shrine, with a canopy of open pillars and many tiers of flowers and candles. Then, waggon after waggon with sides and roof of canvas, so that they are like tents on wheels, but this does not describe their shape, which is that of two-wheeled Gypsy caravans, "expressed," as dress-makers would say, not in wood but canvas. These waggon-tents are decorated and festooned, so that they resemble bowers, and the *majas* sit inside them with their shawls or spotted crinolines showing.

Going at a slow pace through the Triana, among the excited population, there may be as many as forty or fifty of the waggons lumbering one after another....The Romeria lasts for three days, and they encamp beside their waggons. Perhaps it is never so beautiful as when passing under the grey shadow of the olive trees, tent after tent, with its occupants in their Gypsy dresses, and a horseman or two at the back, in stiff grey Córdoban hat and short white jacket, a young girl in a spotted crinoline riding pillion behind him. But it must be wonderful, too, at the evening encampments, when they sing and dance far into the night. And, indeed, song and dance, blazing days, and starlit nights are the attractions of the Romeria.

SACHEVERELL SITWELL, *SPAIN*, 1950

112 On the Monday after Pentecost the statue of the Virgin is brought out of the church by the men of the neighbouring village of Belmonte, and then the fight for the honour of carrying the statue begins, all the cofradias *participating. Men push and claw each other in their attempt to gain possession of the litter on which the statue is carried. All the same, the litter never touches the ground during the five or six hours of the fight, after which the Virgin (grateful, no doubt) is returned to the church.*

For the Spaniards art appears to be regarded as a means to producing particular states of mind. In the main their religious art is really religious as no other European art is....Their art is religious in that it is evidently intended to bring about in the spectator a certain state of wonder, awe, and mystery, a state which is peculiarly suitable for the inculcation of religious doctrine, or at least for the creation of an uncritical reverence for the hidden power behind all this magnificence. The architecture, the sculpture and painting in a Spanish church are all accessory to the purely dramatic art – the religious dance, if you like – of the Mass. By the very superfluity and confusion of so much gold and glitter, guessed at through the dim atmosphere, the mind is exalted and spell-bound. The spectator is not invited to look and understand, he is asked to be passive and receptive; he is reduced to a hypnoidal condition. How different from this is the early Gothic of France or the Renaissance of Italy! In those all is luminous, clear-cut, objective. The mind is drawn out of itself to the active contemplation of forms and colours. Those arts are precisely *expressive* of esthetic ideas – the Spanish is *impressive* by reason of its want of clearness. Its effect is cumulative; it allows of one art mixing with another and all together producing a state which is quite other than that of esthetic comprehension.

ROGER FRY, *A SAMPLER OF CASTILLE,* 1923

Monuments of Faith

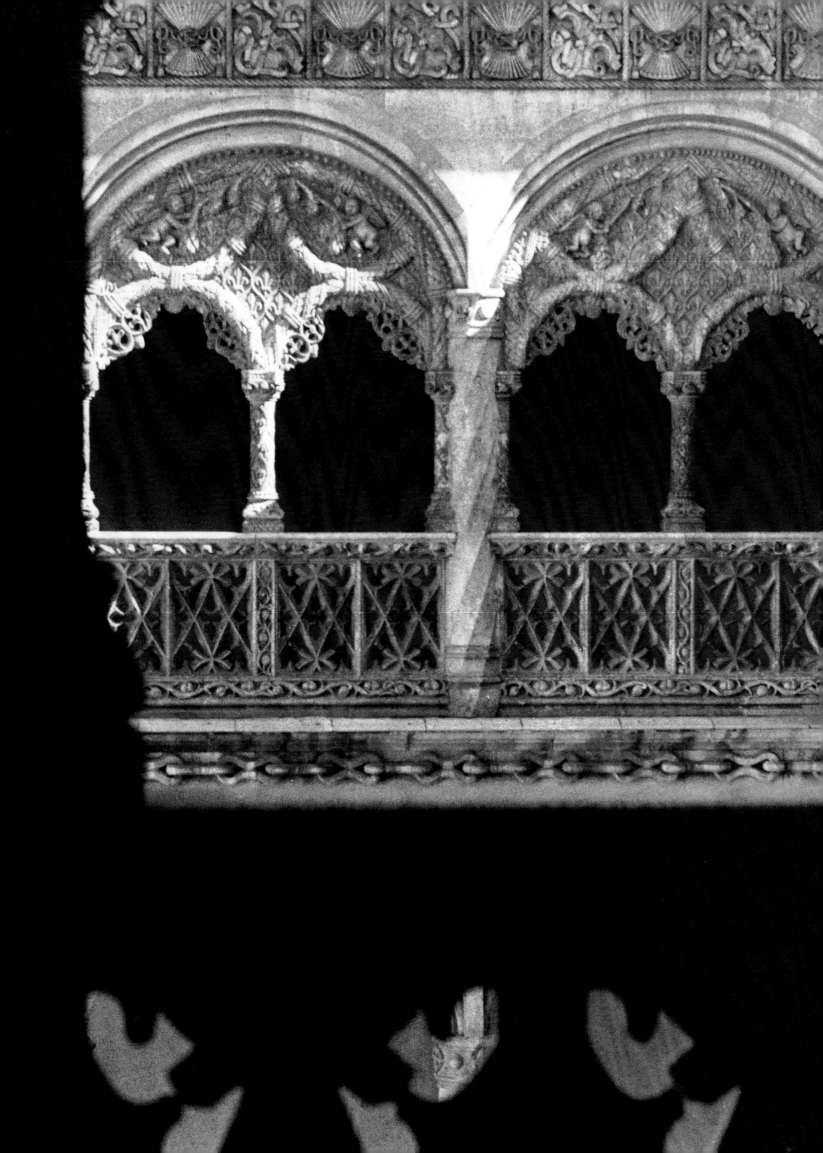

117 A hole in the ambulatory roof of the cathedral at Toledo allows the sun's rays to illuminate the swirling forms on the walls and ceiling. The sculpture in the Transparente, the work of Narciso Tomé, forms a baroque island in this gothic cathedral.

119 The monastery of Montserrat, near Barcelona, was built on the site of a priory that had occupied the spot since the eleventh century. Wagner used the monastery as the setting for Parsifal.

When we have made our way up, beyond even the shrine and the monastery, to the great ravine which is said to have rent the summit of the mountain at the moment of the crucifixion, and when we have passed the fantastic row of rocky pinnacles to which the name of "Guardians of the Holy Grail" has been assigned, we have seen all that there is to connect the real Monserrat with the legendary Monsalvat. Perhaps we should be well content that so sublime a symbol has long been borne away to an invisible home, and that the Holy Grail should have its sole and immortal shrine in the human imagination.

HAVELOCK ELLIS, *THE SOUL OF SPAIN*, 1908

120 The face of the Virgin on the bronze door of the Monastery of Guadalupe has been polished by pilgrims who have touched it before passing through the doors. The Virgin of Guadalupe was the patron of explorers. The documents authorizing Columbus' expedition to the New World were signed here, and it was the first place that Cortés visited upon his return to Spain in 1538.

The climate is so mild here, in Guadalupe, that on the 8th of January the blackbirds were singing in the olive trees, as it happens in Germany in the month of May....We entered the church...it is truly magnificent, with an extraordinarily high dome over the transept....The enormous main altar is made of gold and ivory. In the center stands the image of Our Lady, which was found by a shepherd....We saw innumerable chains that Christian captives had brought here (from North Africa, after being liberated), to show their gratitude to the Virgin, who had helped them to regain their liberty. We also saw a great stuffed crocodile; it had been hunted by some Portuguese of Guinea who had escaped being devoured by the monster when they prayed to Our Lady. There was also a tortoise shell, big enough to have a bath in it, and an elephant tusk and whalebones.

HIERONIMUS MÜNZER, 1495

121 Built in the thirteenth century, the Church of San Miguel, Estella, Navarre, is a striking example of Romanesque art. The tympanum over the main door shows Christ amid the symbols of the four Evangelists. The town of Estella was popular among the mediaeval pilgrims from Paris to Santiago de Compostela in Galicia.

In the land of Spain there is a noble and famous fortified town, which owing to its fair situation, and its fertile fields and its numerous inhabitants, surpasses all other towns in the neighbourhood. It is called Estella.

PETER THE VENERABLE, *DE MIRACULIS*

122 These seventh-century carved capitals from the church of Quintanilla de la Viñas, Burgos, are among the few Visigothic works in Spain that survived the Moorish conquest. Only the apse and transept remain of the original church.

The two capitals represent two angels glorifying Christ. Other sculptured stones arranged along the wall, representing Christ Blessing, or two angels holding a disc with the representation of the sun or that of the moon, are most certainly some capitals of the nave. These figures, whose extraordinary force of expression recalls certain Byzantine ivories of that period, enable us to visualise a Visigothic art, already developed and full of grandeur, destined to be destroyed by the Moorish invasion.

GEORGES PILLEMENT, *UNKNOWN SPAIN,* 1964

123 The Crypt at Leyre Monastery in Navarre was built in the eleventh century with elements from an older construction. When the ruler of Muslim Spain, Almansor, overran Navarre at the end of the tenth century, King García Sánchez moved his court from Pamplona to this monastery. The capitals on the pillars that support the Romanesque church, which is above the crypt, are very close to the ground.

This church is a lovely example of eleventh-century Romanesque: the carvings above the main door should be especially studied.

But the capitals of the columns in the crypt below are two centuries older. They have seen monks of the simpler rule of St. Benedict saying mass before a whole line of kings of Navarre of the ninth and tenth centuries, of whom we know little except their names, and that they were buried here at Leire. They seem shadowy figures from a dim past.

HENRY MYHILL, *THE SPANISH PYRENEES,* 1966

125 Built in the second half of the twelfth century, Santo Domingo in Soria reflects the French Romanesque style. The figures surrounding the portal illustrate stories from Genesis, the Massacre of the Innocents, and episodes in the life of Christ.

126 Santa María de Eunate, Navarre, is a twelfth-century church built for the use of pilgrims on their way to Santiago de Compostela. It is distinctive for its octagonal shape. According to local tradition it once belonged to the Knights Templars, one of the military orders founded in the twelfth century to protect pilgrims on their way to the Holy Land and to Santiago de Compostela.

The Turks fear them terribly. They defend the castles and ramparts, and in battle never flee. But that is exactly what worries me. If I belonged to that order I know very well that I should flee. I should not tarry for blows, for I do not dote on them. They fight too bravely. I do not care to be killed. I would rather pass for a coward and live than to be one of the glorious dead. I would sing for hours for them; that would suit me fine, and I would be very exact in the service, but not at the hour of battle. There I should completely fail.

GUYOT DE PROVINS, 1203-1208

127 The Church of Santa María la Real, Sangüesa, Navarre, was presented in 1132 to the Knights of St. John of Jerusalem. This church is most famous for its façade. The three tiers of the portal represent the Last Judgement, Christ surrounded by the symbols of the Evangelists, and the Virgin with the Twelve Apostles.

129 *Mount Foncebadón in the León Mountains, between Astorga and Ponferrada, was one of the loneliest and most barren passages on the pilgrims' road to Santiago. To encourage the pilgrims through this area, a tradition developed that each would carry a stone and, when reaching the top of the mountain, place it on the pile. During the tenth and eleventh centuries the pile grew at the rate of a half million rocks per year so that it reached enormous proportions, and as the pilgrims went by they knew that they were not alone.*

130 *The richly sculpted gallery of the Patio of San Gregorio Chapel at Valladolid shows the Moorish influence in Spanish architecture, although the chapel was the work of Juan Guas, an architect of Breton origin. It was completed in the last half of the fifteenth century.*

131 *The Romanesque church of San Lorenzo at Sahagún was built by Moorish master craftsmen. There was a great mixture of peoples in Sahagún. According to a chronicle written c. 1140 (attributed in the Middle Ages to Archbishop Turpin, a companion of Charlemagne and Roland), it was here that the French emperor won an important victory over the Moors. The spears of Charlemagne's warriors, who died that day on the bank of the River Cea, were found next morning to have sprouted leaves. This was a sign that the warriors had entered heaven as martyrs. Afterwards the emperor founded a monastery there.*

The French pilgrims in the early Middle Ages were attracted to Sahagún because there the monks were fellow countrymen and a great proportion of the population of the town were Francos, or privileged foreigners. The exaggerated influx of the privileged foreign trades people led to the serious fights which took place between them and the monastery.

WALTER STARKIE, *THE ROAD TO SANTIAGO*, 1957

132 *The Cloister of San Juan de Duero at Soria is part of a monastery founded by the Hospitallers of St. John of Jerusalem.*

The work of art, no less than the other manifestations of the spirit, has this elucidating or, we might say, *Luciferian* mission. An artistic style which does not contain the key to its own interpretation, which consists of a mere reaction of one part of life – the individual heart – to the rest of it, will produce only ambiguous values. Great styles have a sort of stellar or lofty mountain atmosphere through which the refracted life comes forth subdued and purified, drenched in clarity. The artist has not limited himself to producing verses as an almond-tree bursts into bloom in March; he has risen above himself, above his vital spontaneity; he has soared above his own heart and above his surroundings, circling about like the eagle in majestic flight. Through his rhythms, his harmonies of color and line, his perceptions and sentiments, we discover in him a strong power of reflection, of meditation. In the most diverse forms, every great style contains a meridian refulgence and it is like the serenity that descends upon the story elements.

ORTEGA Y GASSET, 1914

Houses of God

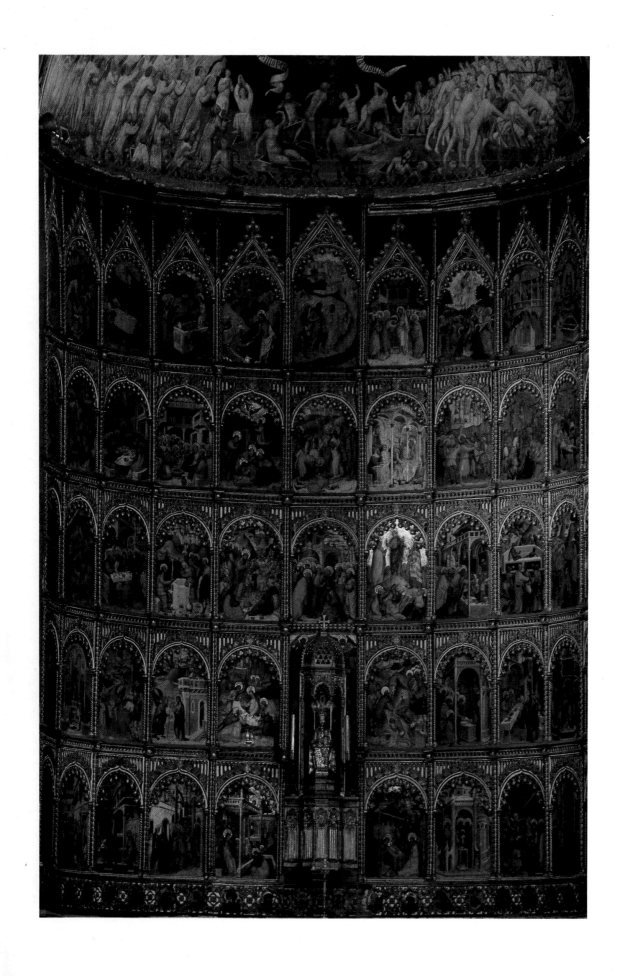

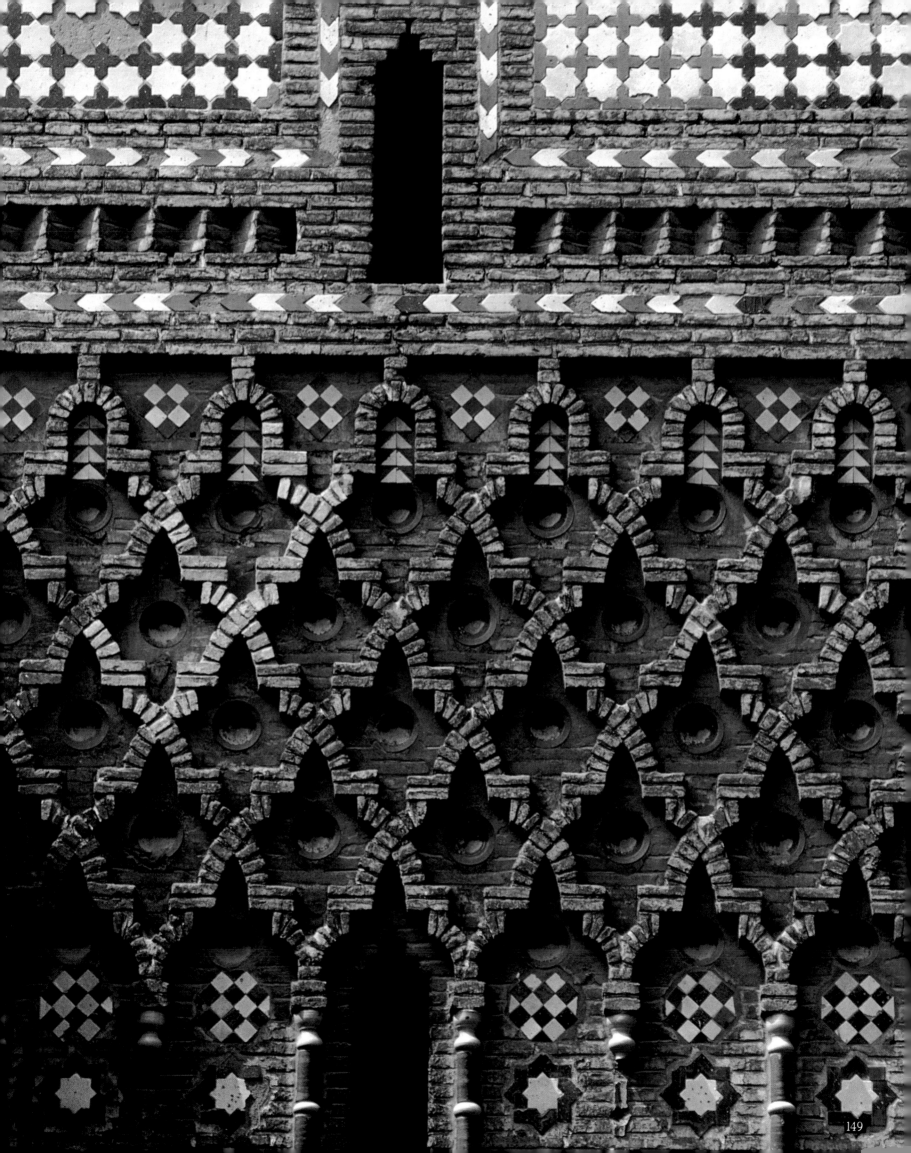

137 Begun in the thirteenth century and completed in the sixteenth, the Cathedral in Burgos reflects the influence of the French and German flamboyant gothic styles more than the other large cathedrals of Spain. The fine stonework and sculpture of the fourteenth century were done by architects and craftsmen who, although inspired by Spanish and Moorish designs, actually came from northern Europe.

Burgos has its Cathedral, which is one of the most beautiful in the world....A huge volume, an album with two thousand plates, twenty rooms full of plaster casts could not give an adequate idea of this prodigious efflorescence of the Gothic style, more exuberant and more complicated than a virgin forest of Brazil...gigantic as a pyramid and delicate like a curl on a woman's ear. It is unconceivable how such a filigree can hold itself in the air after so many centuries. What men were these who built structures that not even the most gifted fairies could surpass?

THÉOPHILE GAUTIER, *VOYAGE EN ESPAGNE,* 1840

139 The Church of the Holy Family (La Sagrada Familia), Barcelona, is the most famous work of the architect Antonio Gaudí. The church reflects the art nouveau *style of the early twentieth century. Construction ceased on Gaudí's death in 1926, but has since been resumed. Covered with a wealth of detail, this unusual structure remains controversial to this day.*

140 Romanesque panel in the Cloister of Santo Domingo de Silos, depicting the Doubting of Saint Thomas.

The Gregorian chant led me from one dream to another without break, for it seemed to underline faintly each thought floating through the mind. It was then that I understood the true significance of such a monastery as Santo Domingo de Silos in the Middle Ages, when life in the world was a medley of bloody battles between feudal barons and their vassals. Within the walls of the monastery peace could always be found for those whose minds had a religious hue and wished to worship God in silence and meditation. Within the high walls there was a paradise of serenity for the artist and scholar, wherein he could express his love and longing for beauty by sculptured figures and illuminated parchments.

WALTER STARKIE, *SPANISH RAGGLE-TAGGLE,* 1934

141 The retable in the Old Cathedral, Salamanca, is the work of a fifteenth-century Italian master, Nicolás Florentino. It is divided into fifty-three panels depicting scenes from the life of Christ and the Virgin Mary. The statue in the centre of La Virgen de La Vega is a thirteenth-century work made of copper, and the throne is decorated with enamel. Most of the cathedral itself is twelfth-century Romanesque.

Through a door leading out of the New Cathedral, down a long flight of shallow steps and there we were, for the *Catedral Vieja* lies within the *Catedral Nueva* like a heart in a human body, a secret, sacred place hidden from the casual eye.

Struck by the strange ceiling spreading like a parasol of stone over you, with imps and goblins, animals and fantastic figures peering down, it will presently become apparent that the stairway replaced a part of the ancient temple. Just at the foot of the steps, a soft radiance enfolds you, for the guide has turned on the lights in a Chapel whose wall is covered with an immense panel showing scenes from the life of Christ and the Virgin. This singular work is composed of more than fifty separate pictures painted on wood, but so framed that at a distance they appear like one picture. Nearly all of them are by Nicolás Florentino, and date from 1445.

MADGE MACBETH, *OVER THE GANGPLANK TO SPAIN,* 1931

143 *An example of the true gothic style, the Cathedral at León was built mainly between the early thirteenth century and the late fourteenth. It resembles Chartres and Rheims in style and has been modified little since the tallest spires were added in the fifteenth century.*

144 *The Romanesque fresco of Christ Pantocrator from the Church of San Clemente, Tahull, is now in the Museum of Catalonian Art, Barcelona. The Church of San Clemente dates from 1123. The frescos are from the same period, but have been removed for preservation. They show very distinct Byzantine origins.*

145 *The Pantheon of the Kings in the Basilica of San Isidoro, León, was painted in the twelfth century on the original eleventh-century ceiling. The frescos have never been retouched and yet retain much of their original vivid colour.*

147 *The Cathedral of Santiago de Compostela, the resting place of the Apostle James, the brother of Christ, was the ultimate goal of pilgrims from all over Europe throughout the middle ages because it was so dangerous to travel to the Holy Land. At its height in the eleventh and twelfth centuries, the pilgrimage attracted more than half a million faithful each year. The pilgrims all followed the same route from the Pyrenees to Santiago de Compostela, along which monasteries and churches sprang up to provide them with services. They brought with them the Romanesque style, which was in turn somewhat modified according to Spanish taste, but which was survived in structures all along the famous route.*

According to legend, the body of St. James was miraculously transported to Spain after his martyrdom in Jerusalem. In the tenth century a hermit discovered a body in a remote spot believed to be that of the apostle, and the shrine that was built around the tomb grew into the city which is now Santiago de Compostela. St. James was declared the patron of Spain and its protector in the wars against the Moors, who were then overrunning the country.

Most of the cathedral was built from the eleventh to the thirteenth century on the site of the original tenth-century basilica. Additions that have been made through the centuries, however, have resulted in a structure that is a blend of Romanesque, gothic, plateresque, and baroque styles.

In the year 1499 the Infanta Catalina was about to be married to the Prince of Wales, the son and heir of the king of England, and she, the daughter of King Fernando and Queen Isabella, before she embarked at Coruña (it was the Jubilee year), attended Mass in the Cathedral at Santiago, which was so full that it seemed as if it would be impossible, without the greatest difficulty, to get another person into the transept. A censer swung above the people as large as a great cauldron, suspended by very thick iron chains. It was filled with live charcoal, upon which had been heaped incense and other perfumes. And it swung so far as to reach almost from one door of the transept to the other. Suddenly, while it was swinging, the chains upon which it was swinging broke with a sound like the report of a gun, and, without dropping a single ash, the censer swung out of the door of the Cathedral, where it was smashed to atoms, and dispersed all its red-hot coals without any one being hurt.

ANNETTE M. B. MEAKIN, *GALICIA*, 1909

148   The most important synagogue in Toledo during the thirteenth century, the Santa María la Blanca Synagogue is a good example of the Almohades style of Moorish architecture. It was converted into a church in 1405.

149   The "mudéjar" style refers primarily to work performed by Moors after the Christian reconquest. The intricate brick and tile work seen on the Mudéjar Tower of San Salvador, Teruel, are typical of this style, which incorporated Christian planning with Moorish building methods and decorative details.

The buildings of the Mudéjares in Aragon have left towns like Calatayud and Teruel more Oriental than European of aspect, and their octagonal church towers and *cimborrios* are features as peculiar to the Christian idiom as are the churches with painted exteriors in the Bucovia....Of the towers that survived until the Civil War, two, according to Mr. Bernard Bevan, were the glories of Mudéjar art. "Both towers," he says, "were clothed in Muslim robes...the windows being divided by terracotta colonnettes, scarlet, green and turquoise. In both towers – San Martín and San Salvador – green and white disks were inset...the cathedral had purple and olive green colonnettes; San Salvador had a roof of white and apple-green tiles; while other churches had tiles of canary-yellow and cobalt blue.

SACHEVERELL SITWELL, *SPAIN*, 1950

151   Begun in the eighth century soon after the first Muslim victories in Spain, this mosque in Córdoba is one of the finest examples of Islamic architecture in the country. This addition to the mosque was made in 987 by Almanzor, Grand Vizier of the Caliphate.

Its walls were fringed with Persian battlements and painted with many colors. Its arcades looked upon a court supplied with ever-murmuring fountains and fragrant with the odor of orange blossoms. Its hundreds of marble columns suggested the spoliation of many a Pagan temple. The ceiling was formed by domes of wood and stucco, whose geometrical patterns disclosed the correctness of taste and inexhaustible fertility and fancy characteristic of the labors of Arab artist and gilder. Its mosaic pavements, its alabaster lattices, its curious arabesques presented finished types of Moorish decorative splendor.

ARAB CHRONICLE

152   Detail of frieze which decorates the exterior of the Church of Santa María de Quintanilla de las Viñas. This church was built in the seventh century by the Visigoths, who used animals and vegetation as inspiration for their motifs.

The sculptures of Santa Maria de Quintanilla de las Viñas have made it one of the most precious Visigothic buildings in Spain. In fact, all along the exterior walls of the apse and the transept there are two friezes – three in the centre of the apse – which are decorated with birds and stylised vegetal motifs, all treated in the most wonderful manner. The decoration forms a series of circles which are tangent to the interior. We can see some lions (at least they are not dogs), gazelles, sheep (at least they are not goats), oxen (which are perhaps bulls), sea horses, heraldic birds, foliage, bunches of grapes, partridge, hens, peacocks, ducks, all related by way of Ravenna and Byzantium to Sassanid art.

GEORGES PILLEMENT, *UNKNOWN SPAIN*, 1964

The "canting" name *Castilla* was taken from the number of castles erected on this frontier of Leon and Asturias, owing to which the Moors called the province *Adhu-l-Kilá,* the "land of the castles," and also *Kashtellah....*The primitive Castilian castles were not the unsubstantial modern *Chateaux en Espagne,* but solid, real defences, and held by brave men, and were built in imitation of Roman fortresses, the noble masonry being quite unlike the Oriental *tapia* (brick wall) of the Moorish Alcazares of the south.

RICHARD FORD, *HANDBOOK FOR SPAIN, 1845*

The Warriors' Legacy

157 *The fifteenth-century castle of Guadamur outside Toledo, where the mad queen, Juana, daughter of Ferdinand and Isabella, sister of Catherine of Aragon and mother of Charles V, lived.*

With tearful eyes he turned to gaze upon the wreck behind:
His rifled coffers, bursten gates, all open to the wind:
No mantle left, nor robe of fur: strip bare his castle hall:
Nor hawk nor falcon in the mew, the perches empty all.
Then forth in sorrow went my Cid, and a deep sigh sighed he;
Yet with a measured voice, and calm, my Cid spake loftily –
"I thank thee, God our Father, thou that dwellest upon high,
I suffer cruel wrong today, but of mine enemy."
As they came riding from Bivar the crow was on the right,
By Burgos gate, upon the left, the crow was there in sight.
My Cid he shrugged his shoulders, and he lifted up his head:
"Good tidings, Alvar Fáñez! we are banished men!" he said.
With sixty lances in his train my Cid rode up the town,
The burghers and their dames from all the windows looking down;
And there were tears in every eye, and on each lip one word:
"A worthy vassal – would to God he served a worthy Lord!"
Fain would they shelter him, but none dared yield to his desire.
Great was the fear through Burgos town of King Alfonso's ire.
Sealed with his royal seal hath come his letter to forbid
All men to offer harbourage or succour to my Cid.
And he that dared to disobey, well did he know the cost –
His goods, his eyes, stood forfeited, his soul and body lost.
A hard and grievous word was that to men of Christian race;
And since they might not greet my Cid, they hid then from his face.

POEM OF THE CID, 12TH CENTURY

159 *The city of Avila is the only completely walled city in Spain. It was recaptured from the Moors in the eleventh century, and these walls were built between 1090 and 1099. They are an excellent example of mediaeval fortifications.*

Decidedly Avila is almost too terrible: granite boulders strew the slopes on which it stands – it rises out of granite and dust and scrub, and rises itself all granite, completely encased in its granite girdle studded thickly throughout the whole circuit with great protruding towers, which come at you with a menace as though they were for offence not for defence.

ROGER FRY, *A SAMPLER OF CASTILLE*, 1923

160 *The fifteenth-century castle of Belmonte, Cuenca.*

161 *The Castle of Coca in Segovia is a masterpiece of mudéjar military architecture built in the early fifteenth century. The castle consists of three concentric rings of fortifications surmounted by crenellated turrets of unusual geometric design.*

163 *Magaña, Soria, a typical small town in Old Castile, where once every village had its own fortifications.*

Then I remember coming out of a gorge one early evening and seeing my first real village. I remember it well, because it was like all Spain, and it was also my first encounter. It stood on a bare brown rock in the sinking sun – a pile of squat houses like cubes of pink sugar. In the centre rose a tower from which a great black bell sent out cracked jerking gusts of vibration. I'd had enough of the hills and lying around in wet bracken, and now I smelt fires and a sweet tang of cooking. I climbed the steep road into the village, and black-robed women, standing in doorways, made soft exclamations as I went by.

LAURIE LEE, *AS I WALKED OUT ONE MIDSUMMER MORNING,* 1969

165 *This foot-bridge below Yesa Reservoir, Navarre, was part of the extensive network of highways built by the Romans over Spain's landscape.*

Rome was to leave on Spain the deepest racial and social influence before that of the Arabs. The Romanization of the country was extremely quick once the military resistance was broken. By the end of the Augustan period Rome had conquered Spain with her arms, and Spain Rome with her letters. The literature of the Silver Age is Spanish. The two great Antonine Emperors, Trajan and Hadrian, were Spanish. Such a swift adaptation suggests not so much an educational as a colonizing effort on the part of Rome. Roman soliders, ex-soldiers, civil servants mixed with the aboriginal population and contributed to Romanization.

SALVADOR DE MADARIAGA, *SPAIN, A MODERN HISTORY,* 1942

167 *Begun in 1238 by Mohammed I, the Alhambra is in a remarkable state of preservation. The palace of the Moorish rulers of Granada, it is particularly renowned for the wealth of its decoration. The delicacy of the carved stucco and ceramic tilework make it one of the masterpieces of Islamic Art.*

L'Alhambra! L'Alhambra! palais que les Génies
Ont doré comme un rêve et remplie d'harmonies,
Forteresse aux crénaux festonnés et croulants,
Où l'on entend la nuit de magiques syllabes,
Quand la lune, à travers les mille arceaux arabes,
    Séme les murs de trèfles blancs!

VICTOR HUGO, *LES ORIENTALES*

168 *The ruins of a castle at Cea in the province of León (beneath the river Cea) lie in one of the grain-growing areas of Spain. In isolated pockets of Spain, little has changed. The wooden sled in the foreground is still used to winnow the grain. The broken stalks are tossed in the wind with wooden forks to separate the wheat from the shaft as it has been done for centuries.*

On the other side of the road, upon a wide space of level ground, I saw a light which must have been ancient when the Pyramids were built. It was a threshing-floor of the sort seen on the wall paintings in the Theban tombs and described in the Old Testament and in Homer. Several farmers had brought the produce of their fields to the floor and the corn was stacked round about ready to be threshed. This was done by threshing sledges moving slowly round on a circular path, driven by boys and men who stood upright, leaning slightly backward as they grasped the reins. The sledges were pulled by mules and as they described their slow circles, crushing out the grain and cutting the straw into chaff, the drivers seen through a cloud of dust had the appearance of charioteers. In Spain, as in the Old Testament, these threshing-floors are well-known places and are used every year at harvest time, indeed they probably have local names that are as familiar in the countryside as the threshing-floor of Ornan the Jebusite, were the Lord halted a pestilence. I was shown one of the sledges, which resembled in every detail the primitive agricultural implement called in *Job* a "threshing wain." It was simply a heavy board whose underside was studded with flints or with iron teeth. "Behold I will make thee a new sharp threshing instrument having teeth," we read in *Isaiah,* "thou shalt thresh the mountains, and beat them small, and shalt make the hills as chaff." This Biblical instrument was known as a *morag;* in Spain they call it a *trillo.* I asked an old fellow whether they ever used a *trillo* with rollers fitted to it, but I have an idea he could not understand me. He replied that they used them in Extremadura, but he may have been trying to please me.

H. V. MORTON, *A STRANGER IN SPAIN,* 1955

169   Watchtowers along the Costa del Sol. These towers were built by the local inhabitants after the Christian reconquest of Spain to warn of Barbary pirates, who continued to plague the coast until the eighteenth century.

171   The Roman Aqueduct at Segovia is one of the finest examples of Roman engineering and until 1906 carried water to the city. Although the exact date of construction is unknown, it is now thought to have been built in the late first and early second centuries, during the reigns of Vespasian and Trajan.

One of the rarities of this country is the aqueduct of Segovia, which is five leagues in length; it has above two hundred arches of extraordinary height, though in several places there are two standing on one another; and 'tis all built on freestone, there having been no mortar or any cement to join them. This is looked on as one of the Roman works, or at least, as worthy to be so.

MADAME D'AULNOY, *TRAVELS INTO SPAIN,* 1691

172   Philip II built the monastery-palace of San Lorenzo del Escorial as a memorial to the Spanish victory over the French on the Feast of St. Lawrence in 1557. He planned to live in the Palace, and he intended the Pantheon to be a tomb for his father, Charles I, and eventually for himself. Philip II's successors continue to be interred there. Construction on the Escorial began in 1562, and was completed in only twenty-one years. Juan de Herrera was the master architect. The huge building contains a monastery, royal apartments, a basilica and the pantheon. It is designed in the shape of a gridiron to commemorate the martyrdom of St. Lawrence.

On coming to El Escorial from the plateresque and in a large measure Churrigueresque Salamanca, the majority of whose overgaudy buildings are little distinguished by simplicity and severity, my eyes are soothed by the pure and rigorous lines of El Escorial, by the proportion and greatness, showing no eager ostentation of this imposing mass.

MIGUEL DE UNAMUNO, *THE LIFE OF DON QUIXOTE AND SANCHO,* 1905

But within the bright walls of its [Spain's] towns and villages it has developed a gregarious and extrovert ritual of life in which there are few outsiders and little loneliness. The Spaniard believes himself superior, both in culture and morality, to any other people in the world, and believes this so steadfastly he neither boasts nor hates but welcomes strangers with a chivalrous warmth based on compassion for their benighted shortcomings.

LAURIE LEE, *I CAN'T STAY LONG,* 1975

Your nation has been called moribund, my Don Quixote, by those who are inebriated with fleeting triumpth and who forget that fortune turns about more times than the earth, and that the very trait which makes us least adapted to the civilization today prevalent in the world may be the quality which will make us more adapted to the civilization of tomorrow. The world turns often, fortune more often still.

We must aspire, by all means, to become eternal and famous not only in the present but in future centuries. A nation cannot survive when its shepherds, who are its conscience, do not conceive of it as possessing an historic mission, an ideal of its own to fulfil on earth. These shepherds must aspire to achieve fame by tending to and exalting their country; thus, while achieving fame, they will lead their nation to its destiny. Is there not in the eternal and infinite Consciousness, an eternal idea of your nation, my Don Quixote? Is there not a celestial Spain, of which this terrestrial Spain is merely a copy and a reflection in the poor centuries of mankind? Does there not exist a soul of Spain, just as immortal as the soul of each one of its sons?

MIGUEL DE UNAMUNO, *THE LIFE OF DON QUIXOTE AND SANCHO,* 1905

Streets to the Past

Spain

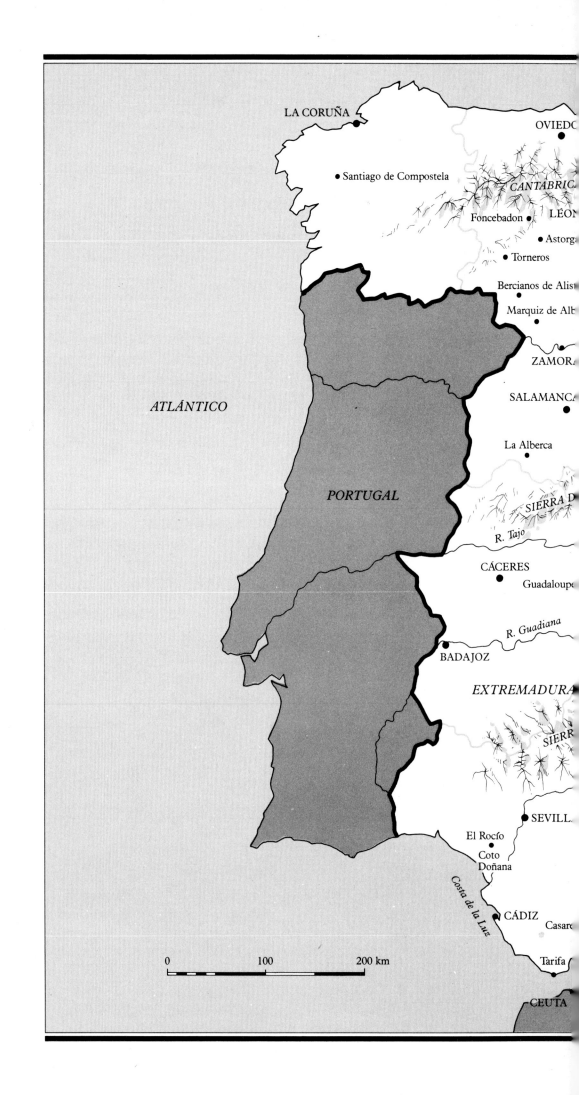

SANTANDER

Bermeo

PICOS DE EUROPA

CORDILLERA

BILBAO

SAN
SEBASTIAN

FRANCE

Cea

PAMPLONA

Puenta la Reina • Eunate
Estella • Yesa • Leyre
Sangüesa
R. Aragón

PYRENEES

Sahagún

BURGOS

Quintanilla de las Viñas
Santo Domingo de Silos

SIERRA DE URBION

Magaña

R. Ebro

ZARAGOZA

Costa Brava

Montserrat

VALLADOLID

SORIA

R. Duero

Sepúlveda

Chodes

BARCELONA

Coca

SEGOVIA

SIERRA DE GUADARRAMA

TARRAGONA

AVILA

GUADALAJARA

El Escorial

GREDOS

MADRID

Albarracín •

TERUEL

Costa del Azahar

Menorca

PALMA

TOLEDO

Guadamur

Belmonte

MONTES DE TOLEDO

LA MANCHA

VALENCIA

Mallorca

Ibiza

CIUDAD REAL

ALBACETE

La Puebla

Formentera

Onteniente

MORENA

R. Guadalquivir

Elche •

ALICANTE

SIERRA DE SEGURA

CÓRDOBA

ANDALUSIA

Costa Blanca

GRANADA

Mecina Alfahar

SIERRA NEVADA

ALMERÍA

MEDITERRANEO

MALAGA

Costa del Sol

AFRICA

Rearing their crests amid the cloudless skies,
   And darkly clustering in the pale moonlight,
Toledo's holy towers and spires arise,
   As from a trembling lake of silver white.
Their mingled shadows intercept the sight.
   Of the broad burial-ground outstretch'd below,
And nought disturbs the silence of the night;
   All sleeps in sullen shade, or silver glow,
All save the heavy swell of Teio's ceaseless flow.

SIR WALTER SCOTT, *THE VISION OF DON RODERICK,* 1811

181 Of pre-Roman origin, Toledo is historically and culturally one of the most important of Spain's cities. A commercial and intellectual centre during the middle ages, it later gained spiritual importance under the Catholic kings and through its identification with its adopted citizen, El Greco, whose famous painting of the city shows how little it has changed through the centuries.

We stopped at last at the foot of a mighty hill and I got out of the 'bus and glanced up. I saw the city of Toledo sitting in the solemnity of the late afternoon, like an old knight with a sword across his knees. The city rose in tiers, a rising mass of roof tiles from which the towers of churches were lifted against a blue sky. It was like a hill town in Italy, but much starker for no cypresses rose from the terraces. The 'bus appeared to gather itself for the supreme moment of its day and, turning at a Moorish gateway, began to grind up the hill into Toledo.

H. V. MORTON, *A STRANGER IN SPAIN*, 1955

182 The Cibeles Fountain is located in the Plaza de la Cibeles, Madrid, at the junction of the Paseo del Prado, the Alcalá and the Paseo de la Castellana. This statue of the Greek goddess of fertility was sculpted in the eighteenth century.

183 The fifteenth-century House of Shells, Salamanca, derives its name from the rows of shells decorating its front wall. The scallop shell is the insignia of St. James, the patron saint of Spain.

We find the five lilies of the Maldonados, those old Capulets of the city, displayed over the entrance of the Casa de las Conchas, built for the family in 1512. The house derives its name from the thirteen rows of shells decorating its front. The most interesting features of the building are the windows, each divided by a slender central shaft, and with delicate traceries in the early plateresque style. Quadrado states that the Jesuits, wishing to acquire the site, offered an ounce of gold for each of the shells, but the owners declined to give up the property at any price.

ALBERT CALVERT, *LEON, BURGOS AND SALAMANCA*, 1908

185 Casares, Málaga, one of Spain's famous "white towns," was first a Roman colony and then a Moorish strong point.

186 La Alberca, Salamanca, is one of the quaint mountain villages located in isolated pockets in the Sierra de la Peña de Francia. The half-timbered houses and twisting, narrow streets which have survived intact make it one of the best preserved mediaeval cities in Europe. The villagers still wear the colourful and distinctive local costumes, especially on Sundays and Feast Days.

But, after all, it is the population of La Alberca who are the greatest curiosity. A number of them sat or stood about under the granite columns. There were old peasants in black kneebreeches and waistcoats, for this was an ordinary weekday; but on feast days there are still remnants of what was once the richest and most beautiful costume in the whole of Spain. It is in this costume, moreover, that there may be discovered the clue to the inhabitants of La Alberca. It is not so particularized in the case of the men, although they wore the widest-brimmed sombreros of the whole kingdom, sombreros with flopping brims only equalled in size by those of the Chod clansmen of the Böhmer Wald, near Domazlice, who guarded of old, the Bohemian frontier with Bavaria. But it is the women's costume of La Alberca that yields the Berber or Mudéjar origin. Unfortunately, it was so valuable for its gold and silver ornaments that it used to be divided at every death in a family and can only with difficulty be assembled again.

The dress, itself, is of heavy velvet with much gold galloon. But the headdress is of white lace or gauze with silk ribbons sewn into it, worn low down over the eyes, and entirely covering the mouth and chin. The other feature is the extraordinary array of necklaces falling as far as the knees, and formed of row after row of enormous gold or coral beads, with rosaries, amulets, reliquaries, and ex-votos, all worn over a sort of golden apron. The characteristics of the costume are the Berber headdress and the enormous necklaces. These were bought from the *charro* jewellers of Salamanca who worked, within living memory, upon these Berber ornaments of the twelfth and thirteenth centuries.

SACHEVERELL SITWELL, *SPAIN*, 1950

187 The Puente la Reina at Navarre was built by Queen Urraca especially for the pilgrims travelling to Santiago de Compostela in the eleventh century.

From Eunate, which incidentally in Basque means the house of the hundred doors, I plodded on to Puente la Reina, the town where the various pilgrim roads from France meet and become the single Road of St. James. Puente la Reina had always been important because it lay on a main road at the crossing of the River Arga, but its importance grew when the bridge was built and the pilgrimage reached its zenith in the eleventh to the fifteenth centuries. In those days the small town gathered people from all over Europe. Lombards, Provençals, Normans rubbed shoulders with English, Irish, Italians, Dutch, Hungarians and Turks. The crowds that gathered in the long narrow streets were not all pilgrims, for the town was known universally as a mart for goods from distant parts of Europe and the pedlars leading their donkeys laden with bales had come from the great commercial cities in Italy and France, following in the footsteps of the Jacobean pilgrims.

As I strolled through the streets of Puente la Reina I felt as if I had suddenly been spirited back to the Middle Ages, for the *calle Mayor* is the actual ancient Road of St. James and the crowds walking along it in the evening towards the bridge at the end of the town make us think of the ancient pilgrims. Then at nine and ten o'clock at night when the church bell rings forty times, the illusion of living in the heyday of the pilgrimage becomes complete, for the forty peals were in the Middle Ages to warn the lonely pilgrim plodding wearily in the night that a haven of rest was at hand. The bells also perpetuate the ancient legend of *La Chori*, which is connected with the statue of Our Lady in the Church of San Pedro. According to the legend, a bird, after moistening its wings in the river, flew one day into the Church of San Pedro and dusted the statue of the Virgin. Hence the title *La Virgen de la Chori* (*chori* in Basque means a bird).

WALTER STARKIE, *THE ROAD TO SANTIAGO*, 1957

188 Albarracin is one of the unusual mountain villages of Teruel. Although much of the construction is of rough stone, many houses in the steep, winding streets have overhanging second storeys with carved woodwork.

Acknowledgements

When developing a book that takes a number of years to produce, there are in the end innumerable people to whom one owes a debt of gratitude. In appreciation I would like to list a few who have directly assisted me along the way and to whom I owe a special word of thanks: Lionel Batut, Madrid; the staff of the Canadian Embassy in Madrid, particularly the Ambassador Georges H. Blouin and Information Assistant Betty M. Hobdey; Adolfo Martin-Gamero, Minister of Information and Tourism, Madrid; the David Kings of Bearsted, Kent; Paul Newbury and Richard Pierre of Toronto; the family of José Reza, Plencia, Vizcaya; Thomas and Sonya Ulrich of London; and especially Francisco Hernandez of Carleton University, Ottawa, who laboriously compiled the quotations in this book; and the people of Spain to whose generosity and warmth I shall always be indebted.

Peter Christopher

The publisher gratefully acknowledges permission of the copyright holders to reprint excerpts from the following works:

Roy Campbell, *Lorca.* Copyright 1952 by Bowes & Bowes, copyright © 1952 by Yale University Press. All Rights Reserved. Reprinted by permission of New Directions Publishing Corporation, New York, agents for the Estate of Federico Garcia Lorca.

Havelock Ellis, *The Soul of Spain,* Constable & Co. Ltd.

Richard Ford, *Handbook for Spain, 1845,* Centaur Press Ltd., Fontell, Sussex.

Ernest Hemingway, "Pamplona in July." Copyright © Ernest Hemingway Inc. From *Byline, Ernest Hemingway,* edited by William White, reprinted with permission of Charles Scribners and Jonathan Cape

Salvador de Madariaga, *Spain, A Modern History,* Praeger Publishers International Ltd.

A. Meakin, *Galicia,* Metheun & Co.

H. V. Morton, *A Stranger in Spain.* Metheun & Co.

Sacheverell Sitwell, *Spain,* B. T. Batsford Ltd.

Images of Spain
Designed by Peter Christopher
Type set by Cooper & Beatty Limited, Toronto
Printed by Balding & Mansell Limited, Great Britain
Bound by Webb Son & Co. Ltd., Great Britain